# CALABASAS GIRLS

*An Intimate History*
*1885 - 1912*

by Catherine Mulholland

**MANY**
**MOONS**
PRESS

Book design by Mark Morrall Dodge.

Cover design and art direction by Hortensia Chu. She also created the Many Moons Press logo.

Production by Richard Burns, Regina Books and printing by Cushing-Malloy, Inc.

ISBN 978-0-9700481-6-5

MANY
MOONS
PRESS
P.O. Box 94505
Pasadena, California 91109

Printed in the United States of America

# Contents

*To*

*Addie Haas Mulholland*

*1896-1980*

*and*

*to the memory of*

*Katie Ijams Haas*

*1876-1968*

*my mother and grandmother*

# Foreword

Catherine Mulholland originally wrote this gem of family history as an eightieth birthday gift for her mother, Addie Haas Mulholland, and it was published in 1976 in a limited edition. But the copies soon scattered as interest in this early Valley history grew. The book provided a vision of people and the land—Calabasas and glimpses of Pasadena—which could be found nowhere else.

This fresh edition of *Calabasas Girls* responds to requests from the historical societies and residents of Calabasas and the wider San Fernando Valley, wanting to have this historical record available once again. The events in the book have receded further into the past, but the sharp details of these family moments remain undimmed. Much of this is the common past of all Southern California towns.

To continue this lively and human history, Catherine Mulholland has also written a set of essays drawn from newspaper and other sources, which appears in the forthcoming companion volume, *Calabasas Lives*. With that work, she completes her chronicle of a lost world, "a Western outpost called Calabasas."

It has been said that time is the fourth dimension. If that is true, we may step into that dimension (which is always with us, after all) and, with the turn of a page, be in those pioneer days once again.

\* \* \*

This book was designed by Mark Morrall Dodge and produced by Richard D. Burns of Regina Books. The cover design is the work of Hortensia Chu. Many Moons Press is grateful for a contribution from the City of Calabasas toward the publication of the book.

ABOUT THE COVER IMAGE: This painting, titled "The Adobe House of Juan Menendez at Calabasas," is by Eva Scott Fenyes (1949-1930), an artist and patron of the arts in Pasadena. The image is dated 1915 and is one of about 300 watercolors she painted as commissioned by Charles Lummis, to preserve the likeness of early Southern California buildings while they still existed. Once the home of Miguel Leonis, the adobe was occupied by his stepson Menendez after the death of Leonis in 1889. Today the building is known as the Leonis Adobe and is the premier historic site in Calabasas. Image reproduced by courtesy of the Braun Research Library, Autry National Center; FEN 199.

ABOUT THE PHOTOGRAPHS: The back cover image shows the Calabasas Post Office and General Store, about 1905, with members of the Perret and Haas families. The photographs in this book were provided by the author..

ELIZABETH POMEROY
Pasadena, California
June, 2008

x

# *Preface*

The following history is based almost entirely on family papers, reminiscences, and the author's personal notes and memories.

The letters, which form the heart of the work, were found among Katie Ijams Haas' effects after her death in 1968 and are in the possession of her daughter, Edith Haas Hull, who kindly loaned them to me and granted permission to use them as I saw fit. To her, my Aunt Edith, I give my deepest thanks.

In editing the letters, I have not Englished the prose, but allowed each writer to keep his own voice and style: Edith Ijams' Southern flavor, Isaac Ijams' flowery rhetoric and old frontiersman's style, Nettie and Katie Ijams' and John Haas' Western American tone. I hope that they will recall the quality of each writer to those who once knew them and present them realistically to those who did not.

Spellings have been preserved except when difficult to understand, or when an obvious slip of the pen occurred. Punctuation has been provided only when necessary to give clarity. For example, Isaac Ijams rarely used a period, which distracts from the easy reading of his flow of words. I have therefore added periods. Omissions have been minor and are indicated by an ellipsis (...).

The letters lead us back to the vanished world of pre-automobile Southern California. For members of the family, I hope this work will be both enlightening and interesting. For those outside our family, I ask that they entertain Montaigne's paradox:

*All men are alike else we could not recognize each other; all men are different else we could not tell one another apart.*

Berkeley, 1976

# Acknowledgments

Thanks go to those who have done research and writing on the pioneer past of Calabasas and to the Calabasas Historical Society whose members have provided invaluable service in the preservation of local history. Thanks also to those descendants of old settlers who have transcribed their records. In 1981, for example, Doris Weber Fredendall completed an impressive document, "Family History of Joe and Carrie Smith," tracing the lives of her forebears who settled there in the 1890s and early 1900s. Her unpublished typescript includes anecdotes of numerous Calabasas individuals and families, including my families of Ijams, Haas, and Perret.

In my years of speaking to historical societies, I have also encountered many who often kindly supplied me with bits of additional information about their own Calabasas ancestors. Beverly Daic Taber, a descendant of both the pioneering Palma y Mesa and Daic families, provided me with an accurate record of their members, while former Judge John Merrick of Malibu once invited me to his courthouse in order that I might see the records made by the Justices of Peace in the Calabasas Township from 1904-1927.

The other champions of historic preservation have been the Calabasas Historical Society and the Leonis Adobe Association, especially under the early leadership of Ray Phillips, who, with his wife Nancy and devoted leaders and workers, achieved marvels in conserving a landmark site.

Finally, I wish to express my appreciation and gratitude to two admirable individuals who made the publication of this work possible, Dennis Washburn, civic leader and former Mayor of the City of Calabasas, and Elizabeth Pomeroy, publisher of Many Moons Press.

CATHERINE MULHOLLAND

2008

## To Calabasas

An area in Los Angeles County which is bounded on the north and east by the San Femando Valley, on the south by the Santa Monica mountains and Pacific Ocean, and on the west by Ventura County.

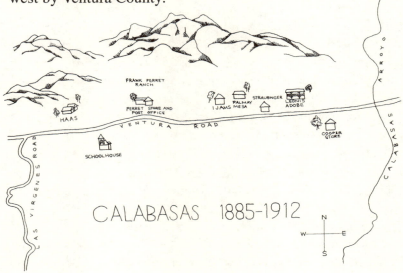

EXCERPT FROM THE MINUTES OF A MEETING OF
HOMESTEADERS IN WHICH IT WAS DECIDED TO RETAIN THE
NAME OF CALABASAS

Chairman:        Calabasas is squashes,
                 Calabozo is jailhouse,
                 And Caboose is the end of the line.
                 Take your pick.

Homesteader:     Reckon we oughta call it by a white man's
                 word?

Chairman:        What you got in mind?

Homesteader:     Pardonin' the suggestion—let's call it
                 Poverty.

# A Conversation

| | |
|---|---|
| Wayfaring Stranger: | Can you tell me some of the outstanding features of this vicinity? |
| Homesteader: | Well, we got dust in summer and mud in winter, not to mention rattlers, tarantulas, bad drinkin' water and a North Wind can blow your upper plate clean over them mountains to the Pacific Ocean less'n you learn to keep your mouth shut. |
| | PAUSE |
| | Yep. We're tough. Got a tough reputation. Worse'n El Monte, and Monte brags how they got one killing per freehold, but I think we got 'em beat. |
| Child (interrupting): | Tell him about the wild flowers. The lupine and poppies that bloom after the rain, The Indian Paint Brush and Mariposa lilies And back in the canyons, maidenhair fern. Tell him there's picnics and Christmas and dances, And the big cattle brandings— |
| Homesteader: | Hush up. You want to give this gentleman here the wrong impression? |

*The Calabasas Post Office and General Store, about 1905, with members of the Haas and Perret families*

# CALABASAS GIRLS

THE THREE FAMILIES IN THIS HISTORY

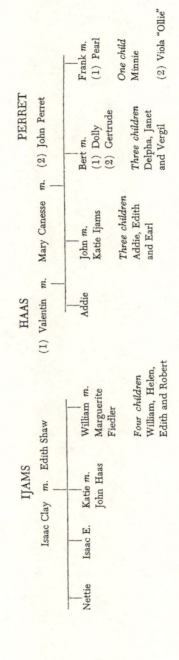

# NETTIE & KATIE
## (1885-1893)

### How The Ijams Came To Calabasas

IN 1885, as Southern California was about to rocket off on one of the wildest land booms in its history, a California family named Ijams trudged its way southward down the coast road from Santa Barbara with a team and wagon loaded with its worldly goods, including the chickens in their crates and the pregnant family cow tied to the back of the wagon. All day they had moved, struggled their way over the rugged, precipitate and formidable Conejo Grade and, exhausted by the rigors of the day's march they stopped, the father having decided to make camp along the banks of a wash which was bordered by good pasture from the winter rains and surrounded by mountains with rocky outcroppings, boulders, canyons, arroyos and an abundance of live oaks on the hillsides. An admirable location for a prolonged camp, thought the father, Isaac Clay Ijams, who had a seasoned eye in such matters, having spent his youth as an adventuring gold seeker, scout and guide over much of the American West.

Isaac Ijams chose with care because he knew that their cow was near her time, and it was important that she have her calf under the best possible circumstances as she was a precious economic asset of this hard-pressed family. In this pleasant spot they could rest, the calf would be delivered,

3

and they would then be in good shape to journey on to their destination in Alessandro,[1] where a job awaited them as caretakers of a friend's hotel. Thus it was that the Ijams made their camp that night in a territory of Los Angeles County called Calabasas.

The Ijams family consisted of the father, Isaac Clay, forty-four years of age, the mother, Edith Camelia, forty-five, and their four children: Nettie, just twelve, Isaac Edwin, ten and a half (called hereafter Isaac E. to prevent confusion with his father), Katie May, almost eight, and William Frederick (Willie), the baby of the family, not quite seven.

They were a lively, healthy family but untouched by prosperity. Indeed, the father, Isaac, seemed to possess a marvelous resistance to making money. You might almost say he had a gift for it. He was a great believer in the doctrine of Manifest Destiny ("Westward the course of Empire takes its way"), but was not a practitioner of it in the grand manner of the railroad tycoons, land barons and silver kings. Where the jack rabbits leaped across the empty plain, they could safely continue to leap so long as only Isaac Ijams watched them. If he had visions of platting the land for the future development of a town and 10,000 homes, of building the tunnel down to the vein which would yield the highest-grade ore, of laying track to put the country on wheels and getting the government to foot the bill, of buying one-third of the San Fernando Valley at $2.00 an acre, if he ever entertained such dreams, he did not act on them. For Isaac, Westward sufficed. The course of Empire he left to other hands.

---

[1] Alessandro, seventeen miles south of San Bernardino, was a town and station stop on the Santa Fe branch line to Temecula and San Jacinto.

He had worked hard at times, but the long dulling grind of daily routine and repetitive labor were not to his taste. Tedious and dull were active words in his vocabulary (he pronounced the former, "tee-jus", with just a touch of d-sound between the two syllables), and he avoided situations which could be described by these adjectives. In Isaac there was little of the ant; he was almost all grasshopper.

Orphaned at birth in Logan, Hocking County, Ohio, and farmed around to various relatives, he began to earn his own living at the age of ten as a farm hand for the princely salary of $4.00 a month. At the age of eighteen, he started West, reaching Iowa City, Iowa, in 1858, where he remained for two years with an uncle, travelling through the state demonstrating and selling the patents of various farming implements. Then, in 1860, "as war clouds were overshadowing our home and not being an advocate of war, I joined a company of volunteers going westward in search of gold and adventure."[2]

Three times he was to make the trek across the prairies and the great American Desert. They called him the White-haired Kid. While the Civil War harvested its destruction of the South and its plutocracy of the North, Isaac Ijams prospected for gold, served as a guide and Indian fighter in Montana, Idaho, Arizona and Mexico. When he rode back to California from Arizona in 1865, he had not found the big bonanza, but he had seen almost all the American West worth talking about.

For the next five years, he worked and prospected in Southern California. When he heard the news of a gold

---

[2]  From a letter written by J.C. Ijams in 1931. Isaac Ijams' full story remains to be told. It is too lengthy to be recounted here.

strike down in Julian City, San Diego County, he went, and there in 1870 met Miss Edith Shaw, who was teaching school at the mining camp and living with her two brothers. The Shaws had fled the ravages of the Civil War and Reconstruction in their home near Shreveport, Bossier Parish, Louisiana. Edith, a little lady with an astoundingly luxuriant head of dark hair which flowed down the length of her body, caught Isaac's eye. Or possibly it was the other way around. On the evidence of the photograph taken at the time of their marriage, he was certainly a handsome man. But he was now thirty years old, no longer the White-haired Kid, and perhaps the thought of settling down with a sweet lady from the South did not threaten to be "teejus."

He must have had his reservations, however, because when Miss Edith suggested to him that matrimony might be desirable, he grandly told her that he would marry her, but not to expect him to change his ways. "So they married," his son Isaac E. told in later years, "and Mother spent her first year of married life under a tree."

Tenting out did not halt true love, however, and before the birth of their first child, Nettie, in 1873, they moved indoors to a rough cabin sixty miles east of Julian near Banner Canyon. For the next eleven years they lived in various locations in the back country of San Diego County, during which time three children were born. Isaac wrote this account of his early married life:

"After my marriage, it was necessary for me to change my rambling into industry so my wife's brother and I pooled our interests, built a saw mill, and supplied the community with lumber necessary to build up the surrounding territory. When the mines began to diminish in value, I followed various interests, added a flour mill to the saw mill, had a bee apiary, and a trading post for the Indians."[3]

Circumstances were not flourishing, however, so when they were invited to go to Santa Barbara to help run a dairy, they accepted. Loading the wagon, off they went. The Baileys who owned the dairy were good friends and had stood witness to the marriage of Isaac and Edith, so that the auguries for the new venture seemed favorable. Hope lay ahead in Santa Barbara, beckoning like a New Zion to the children, now ranging in age from eleven to five, and to Edith, almost forty-five and now possessed of the stony gaze of the overtired, overworked pioneer woman.

For one member of the family, that hope was fulfilled. Katie would always remember her year in Santa Barbara as one of the happiest of her life. Katie was seven-going-on-eight, ready for school. The dairy was near the Mission, and she was enchanted with the tolling of the Mission bells, which seemed to her the loveliest sound she had ever heard.[4] She began school at the Santa Barbara Mission School, a neat little painted building which seemed very pretty after the rough unpainted cabins of the mining towns. Everybody worked but she was given an attractive task. She was delegated to carry milk from the dairy down to the ships in the harbor, Santa Barbara then being a busy port for the coastal sea trade. How she could conjure up in later life the beauty of the cool early morning with the Mission bells ringing out matins, as she drove a little buggy loaded with

---

[3] Letter cited, Ijams, 1931.

[4] In 1884, the Mission was an Apostolic College for the education of novitiates, and in 1885 was granted a petition by the Church to become part of the Province of the Sacred Heart of Jesus, whose headquarters were in St. Louis.

milk down to the sea! And the men aboard the ships who teased and made over her as she made deliveries. Enchanted vistas and memories for the little girl from the dry lands.

One morning, however, while driving down to the harbor, the pony stumbled, Katie lost the reins, the animal bolted, and there was a sickening upturning of the buggy—a terrible accident. She was not badly hurt, but the damage to the buggy was costly and the fright of it lingered. Then there seemed to be trouble with the grown-ups. Papa and Mr. Bailey not getting on too well, fights, squabbles, not good at all. And the talk of an invitation from one of Papa's friends to go and take care of the hotel at Alessandro. She hated the thought of leaving Santa Barbara, especially the wonderful school where she had learned rhymes which she was able to recite to her grandchildren sixty years later, but Papa had made up his mind: the grasshopper was ready to take his next great leap forward.

Once more Edith cooped her "chickings" into their crates and loaded the wagon. At the end of the first leg of their southward journey, the family found themselves ready for a night's sleep on the banks of the Calabasas Wash. Rest was not to be granted them for long, however. Toward morning, thunder claps broke their sleep, and the sky let pour torrential rain.

Drought is the usual nightmare in Southern California, but rain can be one, too, when a flash flood strikes, pouring water down from the canyons and boiling into the washes and barrancas, spilling over and flooding the land. It rained—as if to make up in a few hours for the long months of dryness. The wash flooded and the family came near to drowning. To escape the flood waters they struggled uphill, the tired, half-asleep children dragging soaked tents, wet chickens, pregnant cow and all, bedraggled, sodden and unprotected. It must have seemed the end of the tether.

The Ijams had been observed the night before by a Basque settler named Solatiel Palma y Mesa, and as they struggled in the storm, he came down from his homestead and invited them to take shelter with his family. They accepted gratefully, and a few days later, dried out and rested, Isaac made up his mind. They would not go on. They would settle in Calabasas. He said it best himself, "The land spoke, and I ceased to care to wander on."

*Edith Sikes Shaw, born 1839 in Shreveport, Lousiana*

*Isaac Clay Ijams, born 1840 in Logan, Hocking County, Ohio*

*Marriage certificate of Edith and Isaac, 1872*

## THE HOMESTEADERS

Later Isaac was to give romantic reasons for having settled in Calabasas: exchanging the gold of nuggets and pay dust for the riches of golden grain was one way he said it, but he was given to high-flown talk when the speechifying mood was on him and his Welsh ancestry was at the flood. Many of these things he said when he was old, when, as someone has said, we are editing the life we have already lived. Simple exhaustion must have played some part in the decision to remain. Perhaps Edith bowed her back. She and Isaac were now in their mid-forties, they had roamed so much, the children really did need steady schooling. The kindness of the Palma y Mesa family held a promise of good friends and neighbors. The landscape itself, fresh and glistening after the rain: all this, plus the fact that there was still available in Calabasas government land for homesteading, must have played parts in Isaac's decision to settle there.[5]

No sooner had Isaac chosen a quarter section (160 acres) of land near the Palma y Mesa homestead and staked out his claim than trouble broke out. Isaac E. remembered it this way: "The Big Basque promptly tried to drive us off. He said we were squatters on a Spanish land grant. But he didn't figure on the sort of man my father was. It was government land and my father took his case to court and won out."

A squatter's war had raged in Calabasas since 1870 when Miguel Leonis, the Big Basque or El Basquo Grande, a former smuggler in the Pyrenees who was wanted by both Spanish and French customs officers, had migrated to America and come to the San Fernando Valley. He married a half-Indian woman whose father owned Rancho El Escorpion, a great landholding to the north of Calabasas at the west end of the San Fernando Valley, and as he took control of his father-in-law's herds and flocks, he also began to move them out onto Government land, appropriating it for himself and shooting and scaring off homesteaders as they appeared.

The best account of Calabasas in this period was written by Major Horace Bell in his entertaining, posthumously published book, *On the Old West Coast*, 1930. Full of frontier humor and a Biercean irony, his chapter, "Leonis, the Basque, King of Calabasas," gives an account of the

---

[5] The Homestead Act of 1862 granted a free farm of 160 acres to any person who would occupy and improve it for five years.

squatters' war. Bell himself served as an attorney for some of the battling squatters; indeed, the Palma y Mesa who had succored the Ijams family was represented in the courts by Horace Bell, who won the suit for Mesa and collected damages from Leonis.

When the Ijams homesteaded in 1885, Leonis' star was on the wane, and by the time of his death in the late 1880's, a new bully had arisen to harass the settlers: Harvey A. Branscomb, a self-appointed leader and questionably-elected Constable of Calabasas. A kind of frontier Sheriff of Nottingham, he dominated the scene into the late 1890's. His job as constable operated on the fee system: the more law violations there were, the greater his accumulation of fees. He was suspected of creating situations and causing trouble to increase his income, and whatever the truth of that charge, there is no doubt that he helped keep the settlers in a constant state of uproar and outrage.

Into this cantankerous frontier territory the Ijams settled. On their land not a furrow had been turned. They pitched a tent and lived in it as they built a house of sorts. Katie never tired of telling how her family had come to Calabasas, but as the years went on, the harsh realities softened in the chambers of memory, and her stories, like her father's, acquired elegant variations and touchings-up. The house in Calabasas provides such an instance. She showed me once a short paper written by Isaac as an old man: probably notes for a coming interview with one of the newspaper reporters who visited him annually as his age increased and his longevity became newsworthy, or perhaps it was a speech he'd written out for a banquet where he would be called upon to make a few remarks and instead would deliver a lengthy oration to the captive assemblage on the pioneer way of life. Whatever the case, on this paper he had written that after coming to Calabasas, he had built a shack for his family. Very carefully, Katie had lined out shack and written small house.

In addition to building the shack/small house, the Ijams also rented land on El Escorpion Ranch to start a grain crop, and Isaac looked about for a school for the children. While these activities were going on, one cannot help thinking of Edith Ijams, at the age of forty-six and after thirteen years of married life and four children, back where she had started from: in a tent. Isaac had certainly kept his word to her in one regard: he had not changed his ways.

## Two Sisters

By 1891 the Ijams had been in Calabasas for six years. Like Edith Ijams' chickens they scratched as best they could, but it was slim pickings. They had built a house and by moving and tacking alongside their home an abandoned granary, they also had created a schoolhouse. Whatever teacher they were able to acquire from Los Angeles then lived with them as a member of the family. The ones who came were sometimes not too choice as the salaries were almost nonexistent (as little as two dollars a month) and the working conditions less than pleasant. Failing a teacher, the adults had to step in. Isaac E. recalled that his father used to teach from time to time, "and if a kid started to get ahead of Dad on the subject, Dad just set him back a grade." Katie remembered that the first Calabasas school session had four students and a widow teaching them.

*Nettie Camelia, 1873-1893*

*Isaac Edwin, born 1874*

*Katie May, born 1876*

*William Frederick, born 1878*

Isaac also arranged that the Calabasas Post Office be established at his place, and in August 1888, his daughter Nettie, then fifteen years old, became Calabasas' first postmaster. Isaac himself carried the mail either on horseback or by cart and horse all the way from New Jerusalem to Colegrove (now El Rio and South Hollywood respectively), a journey that could take three days. The Ijams' place developed all the versatility of a one-man band: school children, boarding teachers, letter-writing and package-sending neighbors, a lively assortment of folk made their way to their homestead, not to mention relatives, cronies and just plain droppers-in, because the family was gregarious and unfailingly hospitable.

There was a store nearby, and on days when the judge came out from Los Angeles to hold sessions, it doubled as a courthouse. Isaac, with his expansive nature and legalistic turn of mind, doubtless reveled in the doings there, because Calabasas at that time must have been the most litigious community in all of Southern California. The squatters' wars of the past decade and the dubious activities of Constable Branscomb and his followers had brewed a spirit of distrust and contentiousness which constantly threatened to boil over. The killings had subsided; the distrust had not. Men worked their fields with rifles at the ready, and any suspected infringement of boundary lines or theft of stock or poultry could provoke gunfire or a trip to the courthouse to begin a suit against the suspected offender. Going to court was a chief pastime and recreation, and the social tone of the place recalls Ambrose Bierce's definition of a gentleman as "a man who bathes and who has never been to jail." There was still plenty of "wild" left in the West at Calabasas.

According to Horace Bell, "While male Calabasans are spying on each other and the stranger, the females supply the family larders by hook and by crook and also by raising poultry."[6] Edith with her chickens was a representative lady of the settlement. In her letters we learn that it is her egg money which sometimes staved off desolation and sometimes provided small amenities. It also helped her daughter Nettie to buy a precious sewing machine. Would this hard-working lady have been amused by a contemporary tourist guidebook of Southern California which listed turkey raising as "a novel minor industry in Southern California ?"[7] For Edith Ijams, it could have been neither minor nor novel.

The work of a pioneer family was endless. Without it and cooperation, survival itself was doubtful. Isaac's oft-spoken "Root, hog, or die," could have served as the family motto, and Edith could have added Louisa May Alcott's favorite prayer, "God help us all and keep us for one another." Not for oneself, but for one another; children were not expected to unfold for themselves but were to enter into the business of preserving the family as soon as they were able. Children of the frontier were economic assets to their parents. Needed to keep the family machinery moving, they were welcomed as new helping hands, and they understood that this was expected of them.

Children of the 19th century quickly became "little men" and "little women," with all that those phrases suggest. They were not held as separate creatures from adults but rather as less evolved adults; not so competent

---

[6]  Bell, Horace, *On the Old West Coast*, p. 182.

[7]  James, Geo. W., *Travelers' Handbook to Southern California*, p. 155.

or efficient as their elders, but that was simply a matter of degree rather than difference. Parents were not regarded as villainous exploiters of their young, therefore, when they put them to work, which is what Isaac did with his children. Bear in mind that although the evils of child labor had been fully exposed by many writers from Dickens on, it was not until 1912 that the first anti-child labor legislation was enacted in Massachusetts and that as late as 1924, the Child Labor Amendment to the Constitution had not yet been ratified by all the states.

Isaac Ijams was a man of his times and he had no money. Therefore, he found jobs for his children: the sons, when they were able, worked in their own fields or on neighboring ranches; the daughters performed the endless domestic tasks with their mother, but Isaac sometimes found other jobs for them.

Katie carried one bitter memory to her grave. Katie, who loved and venerated her father, who kept house for him after he and she had each been widowed, dutiful, loyal, who clipped newspaper poetry with lines which read, "Unsung in songs but shrined in loving hearts, My Father," Katie held one memory for which she could not forgive her father:

"When I was fourteen, he sent me to Los Angeles to work as a serving girl. And they didn't treat me right. They gave me gunny sacks to sleep on in the attic and the nastiest kinds of jobs to do. When he came back to see how I was getting on, I cried so hard, he took me home." To his credit, he did take her home.

In the summers the Ijams children worked in the fruit harvests of Los Angeles County. It was too dry for fruit orchards in Calabasas, so they had to leave home to find the crops. The canning of fruit had begun in Southern California in the 1870's, so there was also work in the canneries. In August, 1891, Nettie and Katie went to Newhall to work in the fruit harvest there.

Nettie had doubtless left her childhood behind in the San Diego towns of Julian and Mesa Grande. The first-born daughter of a frontier family bore a heavy load. She had to become her overburdened mother's helping hand as soon as she was able, and there were no options but illness or death. Nettie had fulfilled her role marvelously well. She was sturdy, of a stable temperament, and regarded by her younger sister Katie as an altogether superior human being: "Nettie was a saint compared to me." When the girls went to Newhall, Nettie was eighteen years old and no longer a "little woman" but an adult expected to seize the reins and hold on, while Katie at fifteen could still qualify as a "little woman" and was so regarded by Nettie when she wrote home to her father:

> Newhall, Calif.[8]
>
> Aug. 2, 1891
>
> My Dear Father:
>
> I am very sorry to have to tell you the fruit will not last till the middle of this week, so then our work ends here.
>
> I am very much disappointed, just beginning to make $1.00 per day, and getting settled, when the thing falls through.
>
> There was scarcely any fruit this year, and what there was has not been of the best.

---

[8] Newhall: at the time, most northerly town in Los Angeles County, thirty miles from Los Angeles. A station stop for the Southern Pacific. The girls would have taken the train from San Fernando to reach there and return, going through the San Fernando Tunnel which had been completed in 1876.

I shall not go to Lancaster but will come home.[9]

I never have been so provoked as I was last night. Mr. Brown got here about one o'clock, woke us out of a sound sleep, and then she had to fix him a bed in our tent and you must know how much room there is in it.

They are the "softest" couple it was ever my lot to see.[10] After he had got settled then they talked for about an hour. And Katie and I were so tired and sleepy.

When night comes and we get to bed, we are asleep before 2 minutes. I will write and tell you when to meet us at San Fernando.

It is too bad, we have scarcely made anything. But we have learned a great many things. Never to complain. Never to tell tales on anyone, and treat everybody pleasantly and politely. Not that we have been doing otherwise than this but we have learned them by observation.

We have been treated like ladies, everybody has been so kind and pleasant to us. If we should remain here a month longer, I am sure we should have some very warm friends.

Katie and I have both been homesick today. I have been averaging over 20 boxes per day[11] the past week but Katie has a hard time to get over 15. She got 21 one day, and was so tickled she wrote home to you.

---

[9] Lancaster: the seventh station stop on the Southern Pacific after Newhall. 78 miles from Los Angeles. At that time, it had a population of 85. Probably the girls lacked the money to risk going on and finding that the crop there was also scarce.

[10] "Soft" would have been one of the harshest judgments these pioneer girls could have leveled against a man.

[11] The crop was probably peaches.

I had a letter from Mrs. Branscom yesterday. I will send it to you. You will see we have one dear lady friend interested in our welfare anyway.

Well I will write no more for tonight, and I will expect a reply to this with instructions.

Love to all,

Nettie

In the following summer of 1892, Katie worked in a cannery at Colegrove, now South Hollywood below Sunset Boulevard, but then a small settlement with farms, orchards, a few businesses, a fruit cannery and a post office. Colegrove was the nearest post office to Calabasas until 1893, when a station opened at Toluca (also known as Lankershim and eventually, North Hollywood). While she worked, Katie lived with her aunt and uncle, Robert and Mary Shaw, who had a place west of Cahuenga Pass, probably near the present boundaries of Universal Studios and North Hollywood. The Shaws provided a way station for the Ijams on their trips between Calabasas and Los Angeles, and there was a good deal of visiting back and forth between the two families.

On her first Sunday away from home, Katie wrote to Nettie:

Colegrove

July 17/92

My dear Sister:—

At last I find time enough to drop you a line, as today is Sunday. I would like very much to be at home today. It seems like I have been gone a month although I can't say I have been homesick.

I am kept too busy during the week to think of getting homesick, and today is my first Sunday and I want to write several letters so I'll not have time.

I like my place very much. I have been sorting fruit for the cannery every day but one this week and then I cut.

I get a dollar a day and board myself. But as you know my board costs me nothing so it is clear profit.

You can't imagine how rich I felt when I came home last night with my five dollars and know that I had earned it. That is more than we both earned at Newhall.

Mr. and Mrs. Dedering[12] are very nice people. I like them very much. She is so lively she keeps us laughing most of the time.

There are 10 or 12 boys and four men working there besides myself, Lillie and two Sickler girls.

I have found Lillie Kettle[13] to be a very nice girl. She is not what I thought she was.

I have seen several Calabasas people since I have been here but have not got to speak to any of them long. Mr. Foster got fruit there the other day.

Well now I've told you everything I can think about down here, how is Calabasas?

I suppose it was rather lively there yesterday as I believe that was the day set for the case between (*illegible*) and Mrs. Valdez.

I guess I can get along very well with what clothes I have for the present, anyway till I see how long the fruit is going to last.

---

12 The operators of the cannery.

13 She eventually became Katie's bridesmaid and best friend.

Will said you thought of coming down to get fruit to put up. I wish you would. I think you can get plenty where I am working for a cent a pound. It is plenty good to put up. And I think by staying here you could get other kinds.

Aunt Mary has put up 10 cans of blackberries and 2 of apricots for us. I think that was very kind of her.

We have just been eating a watermelon. It is the first one I have eaten this year.

I want you to write and tell me all the news. It seems like I never hear anything about Calabasas.

Give my love to Bessie, my best regards to Mr. Haas or I mean Jack.[14]

Your loving sister,

Katie

PS . I get up at half past five get my own breakfast and start to work at seven and quit at six. Not very long hours.

Tell Mamma not to work too hard and to write to me sometime. Much love to you all.

Katie

Writing the letter to Nettie must have stimulated pangs of homesickness, and so she wrote a second one:

Colegrove
July 17 / 92

Dear Nettie:—

I have already written you a long letter but I thought I had better write and tell you about your coming to work.

---

[14] John Haas of Calabasas, with whom Nettie was keeping company. Jack was his nickname and he was so called by most of his friends and family.

I would be delighted if you could come but am afraid you are too late. I heard Mr. Dedering tell his wife not to engage any more help for the present. If you had just have let me know a few days previous I am sure you could have gotten a place. The fruit was ripening so fast that Mr. Dedering engaged four men to pick the fruit from the ground and put all the boys to cutting, so he is pretty well supplied at present.

If you come you will have to stay here as they do not care to board any more. I ate my dinner there up till yesterday and then I took my lunch as all the rest of the girls do.

It was real good of you to do that sewing for me.

I would be very glad if Bessie and Tom would stop and see me, or any other Calabasas people. I guess you know how it is when you are away from home. Any one is welcome. I have not got homesick in the least since I've been here. But don't think for a moment I don't think of home for I do quite often too. I have not learned to like Aunt Mary much better since I've been here although she is very good to me.

Give my regards to any inquiring friend, and much love to you all.

K.I.

Six weeks later, Nettie wrote Katie, who was still in Colegrove, and mentioned her imminent departure from Calabasas. She was preparing to go to Ventura to live with James and Mary Stratton, Mary being the daughter of Uncle Robert and Aunt Mary with whom Katie was living. Cousin Mary Stratton had a dressmaking business in Ventura and had invited Nettie to come and live with them and learn the trade.

Calabasas

Aug. 31 92

My Dear Sister:

I have just started to make your skirt but will take time to pen you a few lines.

I have the washing ironing and scrubbing all finished for this week. And what a relief it is.

I went up to see the Settle girls yesterday.

Last night we all went (mamma included) to hear a lecture on phrenology. It was splendid. Mamma enjoyed it very much. He lectured Monday night but I did not go. I think he was rather disgusted with his audience.[15]

I saw Bessie last night, she was very friendly, and is coming down tomorrow to spend the P.M. and will stay to supper. She heard I was going away, and said it makes her feel lonesome to think I was going to stay.

It seems very dull here now Mrs. Newell and Mrs. Mountain were here yesterday . and Mrs. Newell brought me one of her pictures.

I am very glad you are coming home. I do not know what day I will go to Ventura. I had a letter from Mary, she seems anxious for me to come and I wrote to her and told her I would be there Wednesday without fail.

Settles are about to sell out.

Well I must go back to sewing. I will get your dress done by Saturday night.

Love from us all,

Nettie

---

[15] It was either rowdy or lightly attended.

A week later, Nettie had kept her promise to her cousin Mary, and arrived in Ventura. Her first impression of the town was favorable. Ventura in the 1880's had shared in Southern California's land boom with dreams of becoming a great railroad center when the Santa Fe surveyed a route from Santa Monica to Ventura for a railroad line to San Francisco. The boom went bust, however, and the dreams crumbled, but during that period, streets were graded, sidewalks laid, a theater built, and the town assumed metropolitan airs. In 1890, it was lighted by electricity and the population was 3,869. When the vegetable crops (especially beans) were being harvested and shipped up and down the coast to San Francisco and Los Angeles, it was also a lively port. But it had one serious drawback which Nettie encountered immediately: Ventura was and is a very foggy place.

Ventura, Calif.

Sept. 8, 1892

My Dear Folks:

Here I am established in my new home. I cannot yet realize I am so far away from home.

Jimmie met me at New Jerusalem,[16] and we were till after 9 o'clock getting into Ventura. It seemed like I would never get here, and there was a terrible heavy fog. The dew fell off my hat like rain, and unless my hat can be fixed in a different shape I will have to get me a new one, for the fog spoiled it.

---

[16] Now called El Rio, the town was founded by Simon Cohn in 1875 and had a considerable Jewish population. It lies on the banks of the Santa Clara River, 26 miles east of Ventura. "Jimmie" is Mary Stratton's husband.

Ventura is a lovely little town. So far I like it very much, but I have not seen much of it yet.

We have been very busy in the shop ever since my arrival. I shall also serve as an apprentice in the millinery trade. I started in yesterday, but so far I think I prefer the dressmaking to any.

As long as I am kept very busy I do not think I will get homesick. But as soon as I am idle I cannot vouch for myself.

I think there is a very good future ahead for us if the parties in whose hands it lies will only be cautious and careful. Mary has a glowing picture painted out for me, and if she keeps her word I do not think I will regret the move I have made.

I will make my letter short this time, for I am tired, and we have just come in from the street and it is late. I will write you full particulars Sunday. Just wrote this short one to let you know of my safe arrival. Don't wait for my letters though, for I find if we have any work to do we are going to be kept very busy.

I want to hear from home soon. How you all are and how things are progressing.

I did not get the check for my trunk today and fully expected it.

Love to you all and write soon.

Lovingly,
Nettie

Nettie's simple statement, "Jimmie met me at New Jerusalem," scarcely conveys the nature of the journey she

26

had just made either by cart or stage from Calabasas. She had come on the old road over the Conejo Grade, the same one she had traveled with her family when they had left Santa Barbara seven years before, the one on which her father and brother, Isaac E., carried the mail from Colegrove to New Jerusalem. All the family could tell stories about "going over the Conejo," but for all the acquaintance with the road, it could never be said that familiarity with it bred contempt. It was not an easy way: mountainous, precipitate, and in bad weather, downright perilous. Moreover, if one journeyed on to Ventura, there was the Santa Clara River to cross, and in rainy weather this was difficult and dangerous. In 1890, for example, Charles H. Johnson, a rancher in Oxnard, was crossing the river with his family when the wagon accidentally upset, and two of his children were killed.[17]

What follows is a vivid account by a journalist, Josephine Clifford, who traveled by stage down the coast road in the 1870's, and as the conditions of travel had changed little since the time she wrote to the time of this story, I include it to give a first-hand account of "going over the Conejo" by stage:

We had been ascending the mountains for some time, when, during a breathing spell given the horses, the sharp, decided rattle that seems peculiar to just these stages, sounded back to us from somewhere above as though it were the echo of our own wheels. The driver listened a moment, and then broke out with an abrupt oath, for which he didn't even apologize. 'D—that fellow! But I'll make him take the outside.' 'What's the matter?' I

[17] James M. Guinn, *A History of California, Los Angeles, CA*, Historic Record Co., 1907. Vol. II, p. 1677.

asked apprehensively; 'anything wrong?' 'Oh, no!' with a look over to my side of the road where the light of the lanterns fell on the trees that grew up out of the side of the mountainside below us, and were trying to touch the wheels of our coach with their top branches—'nothing at all. Only he's got to take that side of the road and take his chances of going over. He'd no business coming on me here.' The rattling had come nearer all this time and now a light flashed up a little in front of us and directly a fiery, steaming monster seemed rushing down to destroy us. The air had grown chilly and the horses in the approaching stage seemed to have cantered down the mountain at quite a lively gait, for the white steam was issuing from their nostrils and rising in clouds from their bodies. The six gallant horses, reined up short and stamping nervously to be let loose for the onward run, were a noble sight; and the heavy coach, with its two gleaming eyes, was grandly swaying in its springs. Our own horses were blowing little impatient puffs from distended nostrils, and our coach drawn safely up on the rocky hillside. Both of the drivers stopped to exchange the compliments of the day—or, rather, the night, our driver speaking in crusty tones, and, pointing down to where the road fell off steep and precipitous below him, warned the other driver 'not to run ahead of his time again.'

There was nothing remarkable about the supper we took that night except the bats that kept coming in at the front door in a perfectly free-and-easy manner, swarming about our heads till they thought they knew us, and then settling in their favorite nooks and corners. Noticing my untiring endeavors to prevent them from inspecting my head and face too closely, the station keeper observed that people were 'most always afraid of them things when they first come, but that they needn't fright of them; they wouldn't hurt nobody.' The rest of the night was passed inside the stage, though of sleep there was no thought, such jolting and jumping over rocks and boulders; I ache all over to think of it even now!"[18]

A week after Nettie's arrival in Ventura, Katie wrote from Calabasas, explaining that Papa was hunting down her trunk, which had evidently been shipped by rail from San Fernando and gone astray. She also reported that brother Willie, although very sick, would get well, and that she was on no account to come home because of him. Finally, she mentioned that she had taken over Nettie's job as postmaster.

By mid-October Nettie had been gone from home over a month, and the sisters missed each other miserably. The closeness of the family can best be realized by the suffering they experienced when they were apart. Katie, in old age, could still recall the heartsickness she and Nettie felt when they were away from home. Nettie, however, did try to keep a brave front:

Ventura, Cal.
Oct. 17, 1892

My Dear Sister:

Although it is quite late and everyone has retired but me, I thought I had better drop you a few lines, for I have

---

[18] Josephine Clifford, "Tropical California," *Overland Monthly*. Taken from Guinn, Vol. I, pg. 459.

made this a letter evening. But you don't deserve a letter from me, for I have been expecting a letter from some of you for a week.

Well I am just beginning to get reconciled again although I quite often feel a pang of homesickness.

Yesterday I was very sick all day. But feel better today. It is awful cold up here. I very near freeze all the time. Our sewing has just about run out. Cousin Jim went to the Ojai this morning to work.

Mary has done nothing but growl this week.[19]

I had a letter from Mrs. Branscomb this week. I was so surprised. She says she is much better in health since she went up there. Do not tell Branscomb that she wrote to me.

I heard some fine music tonight by the band. There is some kind of a political meeting going on.[20]

How are politics at Calabasas?

Are you going down to the dance Sat. night?

Tell Flora I intend to write to her soon.

You cannot imagine how much I would like to be home tonight. But do some of you write soon. With love to you all.

> I am
>
> Your loving
>
> sister
>
> Nettie

I would write more, but it is late and I am sleepy.

---

[19] Mary was in the early stages of a pregnancy.

[20] An election year: President Benjamin Harrison, Republican vs. Grover Cleveland, Democrat.

In late October, Katie went to Ventura to visit Nettie because there was a plan that she would eventually join her sister there to learn the dressmaking trade. Nettie even dreamed that the two sisters would someday have their own business. Once there, however, Katie became so unhappy and homesick that she left Ventura ahead of schedule and created the jumble of misfiring arrangements which she describes in the letter below, written from New Jerusalem (El Rio), where she is stranded for lack of transportation to return her home. Her difficulties were compounded by rain. The winter of 1892-93 was wet—26.26 inches—a lot of water for Southern California.

New Jerusalem
Nov. 6-92

My Dear Sister:—

I wrote a postal to you this morning, but I did not get it to the office in time to go off on the morning stage so as I have yet a whole day before me I will employ myself for a while writing you what has happened since I left you.

Well, I got across the river all right.[21] The driver had set a lantern on this side of the river just where he wanted to cross. Although the river was pretty high I was not so scared when I was in it as I was before I arrived there.

I came straight here and secured a room and then I went to the P.O. and learned that the mail had arrived early and that two of them had come on horseback and had gone on to Ventura.[22] The Postmaster said he thought one

---

[21] The Santa Clara River.

[22] Isaac E. and a friend had come from Calabasas carrying the mail and had planned to go on to Ventura to visit the sisters. One gathers that brother Isaac was not too pleased to find his sister in New Jerusalem.

of them was my brother and the other was a small man with a dark moustache, which I at once thought must be Huber, and afterwards found I was right.

I had not been here long till they came back and the Postmaster sent them here as I had asked him to do. I was very glad to see them. They had started to Ventura but gave it up after getting to the river.

Everyone is all O.K. at home as far as I questioned.

It was impossible for me to go home today as they had no cart and they thought they could not get a harness even if they got a cart here. Isaac thought the roads would be better by Thursday and that I had better wait here. So I gave way, as badly as I wanted to go home.

Isaac thought I had best go back to Ventura, but I told him "no." I had got this far and was not going to go back. So I'll stay here till then.

I don't think it will cost much to stay here. Would send your money back but think I had better wait till I find out for sure.

Well, this is after supper.

There was a couple of Spanish men came in and played and sang some Spanish songs very nice. I think Mrs. Alvos[23] told one to sing in English. For he did sing a couple of beautiful songs. One was the one you heard me hum-Viz: When A Boy I Used to Dwell, and the other one I don't remember, but it was very pretty. He played the chords on the guitar.

Well, I haven't told you the most exciteable thing that has happened yet. Last night about three o'clock I was awakened by Mrs. Alvos shrieking like she was being

---

[23] The innkeeper. Katie did not speak Spanish, although Isaac E. did.

killed. I could not think what was the matter until she went to one of the men's doors and told him to get up quick that her husband had a spasm of the heart and she wanted him to help her hold him down. It seems that he is subject to these spasms and while he is in one that he is just like a man in a fit. She says if he was allowed he would tear himself to peaces. It took 4 men to hold him last night. But he is much better now.

One man grabbed his coat and pants and struck out down the street. Huber and Isaac slept here too and Mrs. Alvos said they was standing in the door ready to run.

But it was too cold for me to get out of bed. Especially after I found out what was the matter as I knew I could do no good. So all together I put in a very poor night.

I feel rather nervous this evening as there is no one here I know and there seems to be such a tough crowd here now.[24]

Well I think I have written most everything that has happened so far. So will close with much love and kisses to you and love to Mary.

Will not close this tonight so if anything strange or wonderful happens between this and morning will let you know.

Good By, hope we will see each other very soon again.

Katie

Wednesday morning: Nothing new.

Katie

---

[24] Katie's fears were not unfounded. Tough customers were to be found along the road. In 1886, Arthur J. Draper, an English immigrant and a rancher in Simi, Ventura County, was attacked and robbed by desperadoes who had followed him and his brothers on the old coast road all the way from Los Angeles to Soledad, Monterey County. Guinn, Vol. II, p. 1974.

Katie must have returned home safely and been forgiven by all, for a week later she received a friendly newsy letter from her sister:

Ventura,

Nov. 13, 1892

My Dear Sister:

Although I am in a very poor writing mood today, I thought I would pen you a few lines to tell you what I have been doing the last few days.

We had a dress to make by Sunday and we could not get it finished only by working of nights, so we sit up late two nights and get up early of mornings and we had to work on it some this morn before it was completed.

Last night great excitement prevailed. The Democrats had a grand rally. Hurrah! for Cleveland. I just wished you were here last night. They had a parade and a great many fireworks. Some good Democrat gave every little boy in town a tin horn, and it was almost enough to drive one crazy with the noise. After the parade we went to the hall where the successful officers made their speeches.

One man had a magic lantern and every time one of the speakers mentioned Grover Cleveland or Stephenson (sic), they flashed his picture on the wall, and then the cheering was deafening and the fun of it was that everyone in the house that had one of these horns would blow them during the applause. Well, it was exciting. The Stratton family are all black Republicans and we have some pretty hot arguments sometimes. Well, they are so black that I scarcely ever make it a point to go into a very hot argument with them. We got home from the rally at ten, and sit up to sew on that dress till very near one, so I feel pretty bad, it is almost equal to being up to a dance only you lack the pleasure.

I do not think Ventura a healthy place for those that are troubled with throat, lung or head trouble. I notice I felt much worse with my throat and head the last few days, and Cousin Jim and the boys all have Catarrh, and they are very much worse here. Jim was home last night but left for his work again this P.M.

We have no dresses in now to make. But I do not suppose we will be without long.

Has everyone settled down again since the Election? It makes me so mad whenever I think about it.[25]

I guess Mamma feels highly elated over the presidential election. I guess she got the man she wanted. It makes Mary so mad because they make a fuss over Baby Ruth.[26] She calls the democrats fools. I get hot too sometimes but manage to hold my tongue.

Well, dear, I think I must close now. I feel so tired. I will have to rest some for tomorrow.

Hoping I have a long letter containing all the news soon.

> Love to you
> all, your loving
> sister,
> Nettie

Three days later, Nettie wrote to her mother:

---

[25] The Branscomb forces had won again in Calabasas.

[26] Known now only as a candy bar, Baby Ruth was Grover Cleveland's young daughter and the subject of much publicity in an election year.

35

My Dearest Mother:

Although it was such a short letter that I rec'd from you yesterday, still it was very much appreciated by your little girl, who had began to wonder if you had forgotten that she always looked forward to your letters with such pleasure. I also expected one from Katie, and missed her letter very much for it does not seem Tuesday when I do not get a letter from her. But I suppose she was very busy. I often wonder Mamma if you think as I do. I often think that I ought to be at home helping you do the work, then again, sewing is something one can make an honorable living at and any girl can be proud that is a good sewer, so if it should be I had to depend on my own energies I would have something I need never be ashamed of. I assure you it is not near as pleasent a life I lead now as it was at home. But we always have to take the "bitter with the sweet." I am very anxious to teach Katie now. Well I guess my air castle is not very interesting to you.

I have been feeling very poorly the last few days. My head feels awful bad tonight.

I just finished that woman's gloves this evening, and they look very nice.

I made the acquaintance of a very nice old lady here. Her name is Mrs. O'Neil and she lives at the Anacapa Hotel. We made a dress for her and I went to church one Sunday with her.

Well mamma you do not know how surprised I was to hear that the last payment had been made on my machine.

I think you have a bigger claim on it now than I have.[27]

We have not had a dress this week until this evening.

You do not know with what pleasure I look forward to my visit home which will not be until Xmas now but that is not far distant—and I could not very well make a visit sooner.

I guess you are highly elated over our triumph in presidential election. I am sure I am. I attended a political meeting of triumph Sat. night and I am sure the crowd contained no one more enthusiastic or clapped their hands with more vigor than I.

Well Mamma I will stop my chatter for tonight. Hoping to receive a longer letter much sooner than the last. I am ever

Your loving
daughter,
Nettie

Much love to you all

In late November, Katie made a second journey to Ventura, and once more repeated the earlier sequence of events: homesickness and a flight back to Calabasas ahead of schedule. The following two letters tell the story:

Ventura, Cal.
Dec. 1, 1892

Dear Papa and Mamma

Picture your two little girls in a little damp room way up here in Ventura, looking so blue and homesick they do

---

[27] Edith's egg money helped buy the sewing machine.

not know what to do with theirselves and you will have as true a picture as you want of our situation.

Katie is here and does not know what to do, and is more than anxious to know how to get home. It has been raining here hard most all the time since Sunday. She is afraid if she goes to New Jerusalem she cannot go down on the cart. We thought we would surely hear from some of you today.

I hope you are all well, and that Mamma will not have so much to do that it will make her sick.

This has been a glorious rain for the country. I suppose you are quite elated over it. And all the farmers at Calabasas have a smiling countenance.

Last week Mary and I were rushed to death. We made 3 dresses in one week. We would get up at 5 in the morning and sew until 10 at night. I was completely worn out by the time Sunday came and this week we have not had a dress. So that's the way it goes.

I am looking forward very anxiously to my visit home. I am counting the days now. Well I have nothing more of interest to write tonight—so with our love and hoping to hear from some of you soon I am

> Your
> affectionate
> dau—
> Nettie

I have worried so much about Mamma. I am afraid she will have too much to do and make herself sick. Katie says be sure and write next mail and tell her what to do.

Ventura,
California
Dec. 7, 1892

Dear Katie:

I got your letter today What a shame we could not have
had patience and waited till Tuesday's mail and all would
have been well.

Well Katie maybe you think I have not had a picnic of
it today and yesterday. That walk Mary took with us to
the depot when you left just about did her up. I never
did hear anyone complain as much as she has today and
I am just about wild tonight.

*There follows a paragraph containing some instructions
about the post office in Calabasas.*

When you see Jack I guess he will have something to
tell you.[28] I am coming home as soon as possible. I send
some Rose slips.

Love to you all,

Nettie

The Ijams family was reunited for Christmas, 1892,
Nettie and Jack announced their engagement, and after
a prolonged stay, Nettie reluctantly returned to Ventura
only to discover that she would have been better off had
she stayed at home:

---

[28] Nettie and John "Jack" Haas were to reveal their engagement at Christ-
mastime.

Ventura, Cal.
Jan. 24, 1893

My Dear Sister:

Arrived here all safe at 9 o'clock last night. The trip was pretty hard on me. I feel twice as bad tonight as I did last night.

We got in to New Jerusalem at a little past 4. I went over to Mrs. Alvos' to wait for the stage. She gave me a nice warm supper without charging me anything.

Cousin Jim and the boys were at the depot to meet me.

Jim starts for San Luis Obispo in the morning and the rest intend leaving here in a month's time. Mary wrote me a letter last week telling me all about it, and if I had got it Saturday I should not have come back.

Mary has got nothing in the shop but a couple of dresses for her self.

I think Cousin Jim would like me to stay till they find something definate.

But I will let you know soon how soon I will come home. It will not be long I assure you.

I got a letter from Mrs. Branscomb today. She says she would like to hear from you.

Well Katie I will have to make my letter short tonight. I feel so bad, but will write again soon. So with love to you all I am your affectionate sister,

Nettie

Katie to Nettie:

Calabasas
January 26,
1893

My dear Sister:

I suppose you are delighted to be back in Ventura during this lovely rain. When I think of you away up there caught in the rain it makes me think of my own experiance only, of course, it is not quite so bad as you can do more than I could from the fact that you are more accustomed to their ways and have the natural ability of turning out work, something which I very unfortunately, do not, nor I am afraid never will possess. But I suppose everyone has some falt or falts and that is just one of my many.

Well my dear sister, I hope that you did not suffer from lonesomeness as this poor child did. I cannot tell you my feeling for the first few days after you went away, only I know I felt more than I'd like to show.

After so much excitement it made it harder, and then, to cap the climax, I went down to Bessie's at recess on Monday and what do you think she told me? I am sure you could never guess, unless you'd say she was going to be married, but it is not that: it is far more sad. But, there—I'll not keep you waiting in suspense any longer. She is going back east in a very short time, maybe in two weeks.

She was very much distressed because you did not stop. She thought you might be mad because she did not go to our dance. I made all the apologies I could and told her you probably would try and come back before she left. She said she would not have you do that, but maybe her and Tom would go up and see you. It will be a great loss to the neighborhood to loose them and I am sure there are none but will regret their leaving.[29]

Everything is quiet here now. I have seen no one of any importance to talk to since you left.

There has been an agent[30] staying here for a few days but went to town this afternoon. He will be back next week.

Well, I suppose you are trying to decide what to do. I guess you'll not find that very diffacult as there is but one thing to do that I can see. I am not going to advance any advise for in the first place, I am not capable and the second that you did not ask me and probably would not thank me for it.

But I do so want you at home that it seems to me it ought to be enough to bring you back. Although I know I am not always as I should be, I hope I am never so bad as I sometimes seem.

Well, dear, this is rather a dry, prosy letter and I think the best thing I can do is to bring it to an end. I will not write again till I get a letter from you stating what you are going to do, which I hope may not be long.

I am as ever
your devoted
sister,
Kettee

Papa thinks Jim is doing a bad thing going to San Luis Obispo.

---

[29] The Settle Family.

[30] Probably from the postal service in Los Angeles.

Nettie to Edith Ijams:

Ventura

Jan. 29, 1893

My Dear Mother:

I have been writing letters all morning and do not think I have finished unless I write one to you.

I wrote to Katie last night, and I suppose you will receive them both at the same time.

I cannot find much to write about, for I have only left the house once since my return.

Jim has not got off yet for San Luis Obispo, but intends going as soon as the weather will permit, provided he does not get a job before. He has not had a bit of work for two weeks, neither has Mary, and they are quite discouraged.

I said to them last night there was no use in me staying here. But he wanted me to stay till he got up to S.L.O. and they knew what they will do.

I want to get home before Bessie leaves if I can. I hardly know how to come home. If I thought it would not be too much trouble I would come by way of S. Fernando.[31] But I will leave that for Papa to decide on.

There is no use trying to advise Jim and Mary, they are bound to go north and will not listen to anyone.

I suppose you are all glad to see this rain. I am sure it

---

[31] The most comfortable way, but someone from home would have had to drive to San Fernando to fetch her.

43

will do lots of good.

Well Mamma I have written about all that there is to write. So with much love to you all, and write soon too.

Your loving daughter,

Nettie

Nettie to Katie:

Ventura
Feb. 5, 1893

My Dear Sister:

Your letter and Papa's postal rec'd last evening. I would like so very much to come home on Wed. but could hardly do it after telling Jim I would stay with Mary until he got to S.L.O. She had a letter from them yesterday and they were only as far as Carpenteria. So no telling when they will get there.

I have been feeling very poorly this last week, and will be so glad to get away from this dirty little hole.

Mary is sick too this morning.

It rained here all last night, but is clear and nice at present.

We do not have a thing to do only what little cooking there is from one day to another. So it grows very monotonous for me.

Now about coming home as I am not certain when I can come. I shall go home on the mail cart so it will not put anyone out. Although I dread the trip very much that way. But I want to come as soon as Mary hears from Jim. I shall ship my trunk C.O.D. to Fernando.

I guess some of you will have to send me a dollar for I have not enough money to get home with.

Well dear I will close. Hoping to hear from you soon.

Love to you all I am as ever

> Your loving
> sister,
> Nettie

Nettie to Edith Ijams:

> Ventura
> Feb. 7, 1893

My Dear Mother:

I suppose I had just as well plunge into the subject at once that pains me so much to write about. That is, I have been very sick, had to have the Dr. Now perhaps you think I have caused an unnecessary expense, but I assure you that I had to have one. I cannot explain the nature of my sickness until I see you. But it was caused by taking severe cold. None of you can realize what I have had to go through.

But I am on the improvement now, and hope to be all right the last of this week. I am not confined to my bed, but am too weak to get about much.

Now Mamma what I want to ask you is to spare me five dollars.

You do not know how it pains me to ask it knowing how very hard pressed you are, but I see no other way. I told the Dr. that I was poor and he would have to be lenient with me. And I hope to repay it all some day.

Mary has not heard from Jim yet. She is sick in bed, the Dr. has been here off and on all day waiting on her. She is undoubtedly very sick.[32]

I could not go off and leave her now, for then she would have no one to wait on her and no money to hire any one.

In writing to you about Mary, she does not want Aunt[33] to know of her sickness under any consideration, as you know Aunt is excitable and would flounce up here, cause unnecessary expense. So please do not mention it to them, as we get along very nicely. The Dr. says I will be all right in two or three days. When we hear from Jim if Mary's condition is no better we will telegraph for him.

I hope it will be so I can come home some time next week. And of course I can explain things to you a great deal better there than I can now.

I do not want you to worry one bit about me. I am so sorry that I had to ask you for the money.

So now I will close for I must send this to the P.O. so you will get it as soon as possible. Hoping you are all well.

I am your
Affectionate
Daughter,
Nettie

P.S. I am not one bit afraid to stay with Mary, for if it comes to the worst, she will go to the hospital. I will write you next mail day how she is.

Nettie

---

[32] Mary was also in the final stages of her pregnancy.

[33] Aunt Mary Shaw of Toluca, Mary's mother.

With this poignant letter Nettie's correspondence stops. Somehow she came back to Calabasas. There is no record of how she returned. The cry for help that is implicit in her last letter must surely have bestirred her father or brother to go to Ventura and bring her home (I seem to have a faint memory—or is it only wishful thinking?—of Katie saying long ago, "When we found out how sick she was, Dad brought her home."). What we do know is that less than a month later she was dead. Nettie Ijams died in Calabasas on March 4th, 1893.

Who can measure another's loss? After the death, what can be said to the living? One kind lady in Ventura tried in her plain fashion to console Katie for the irreparable loss of Nettie by composing a letter which first spoke of matters pertaining to the living. It must have brought some comfort because Katie kept it folded among Nettie's letters for the rest of her long life.

Mrs. Webster to Katie:

(Undated)

Dear Katie:

I should have written a second letter to you long ago if I had not been so busy and I hope you will excuse me if I have seemed negligent. Anna is not with me any longer except to lodge at the house and part of the day on Sunday so I have a double portion to attend to.

Mary Stratton has a little daughter named Wilda Bard in honor of her nurse and Dr. respectively. She is doing finely and the child is a week old tomorrow the 4th. She will go to Mr. Stratton as soon as able to stand the trip—probably in about a month.

She suspected or else heard of Nettie's death (by way of

someone else) and questioned and fretted to her nurse till she worried the facts out of the nurse and though I have seen her and spent an hour with her once since she knew it, neither of us mentioned the subject. I did not care to and I do not know how she feels.

Mr. Stratton has rented a place, has a cow, chickens and pig and they will be quite comfortable I hope when she gets ready to go to housekeeping. Dr. H. inquired about Nettie soon after she left but has never mentioned her since. I wish I could know what her physicians said who saw her last. Mrs. Hopkins told Anna that the Dr. did not think she would get well when she left here but I do not believe it (for you know how anxious I felt and how I tried to have him admit that she was in a worse condition than he assumed her to be—but he repeatedly assured me that I was over anxious and he saw nothing in the way of her recovery—and I think if he was secretly doubtful about her recovery that he must have favored her going home because he did not want to admit he did not understand her case. He has acted a little queer about it.)

Did Nettie ever say anything that would lead you to suppose she thought she might not get well? Did she have any signs of Typhoid?[34]

Anna is now in business for herself and is keeping a store for selling cakes pies puddings bread baked meats beans

---

[34] Nettie's death was attributed to consumption, but the true diagnosis of the cause of Nettie's death will remain unknown. The combination of inadequate diagnostic techniques and women's Victorian reticence to discuss certain physical matters obscure the facts of the case. She certainly had respiratory problems, and it may well have been tuberculosis that killed her. Katie once confided that her sister suffered hideously from "female complaints" (dysmenorrhea?), and that at the time of her death, she also had an infection in her female organs. The whole question is academic, but it was almost certainly not typhoid.

etc. and also gets one meal (at noon) for 25 cts. each. She has about 15 boarders to dinner regularly and sometimes as high as 25. This clears her beyond all expenses $25 per month and something over. She does all her own cooking but keeps a girl from 9 o'clock am. till 3 p.m. at $15 per month. Her rent is $12 per month and she has water rates to pay etc. etc. She is learning something of practical business and is getting her eyes open in many ways.

I had packed all of Mrs. Stratton's things and they were nailed up and in such a shape I could not get Nettie's pillow but I have her comfortable and blanket and will send them any time unless you think you or your father and mother may sometime come and get them. I was sorry about the pillow but did not know she had one there till too late.


*In a very small script at the top of the first page over the salutation*


I know you must all feel very lonely and I often wish I might see and talk with you. All our experiences are furnished by our Father Who knows what is best and we all feel that the next life is better than this and Nettie has been called to its enjoyment a little in advance of us only and we shall soon join her. Let us not mourn that she does not linger to partake of any more of this life's burdens.

God bless you all,

Mrs. Webster

*I miss Nettie so much that no one but He Who gave and took her knows how all her early life clusters around my memory.*

Isaac C. Ijams,
1894

*I remember Nettie's grave with a little wooden fence around it at Grandma's and Grandpa's place.*

Addie Haas Mulholland,
1976

# KATIE & JACK
## (1894-1895)

### CALABASAS MEETS PASADENA

ELEVEN MONTHS after the death of Nettie, her former fiancé, John "Jack" Haas, became secretly engaged to her sister, Katie Ijams. John, or Jack as he will be called in this narrative, was born June 19, 1867, in Santa Clara County, the second child of Valentin and Mary Canesse Haas. At the age of five he was abandoned by his mother when she eloped to Australia with John Perret, taking with her Jack's older sister, Addie. A friend of the Haas family, Emma Schenkel of Alameda, California, took the little boy into her home and cared for him until he was old enough to work and live with his father. After Mary Perret had returned from Australia and borne two more sons, Bert and Frank, there was sufficient reconciliation between the parties so that Jack visited with them for brief periods in Altamont, Alameda County, in 1883 and 1884; by then he was a young man of nineteen, living with his father, Valentin, in Milpitas, Alameda County, California.

Who were Jack Haas' parents? There is precious little information left to satisfy a healthy curiosity. Here are the known facts:

VALENTIN HAAS

1. He was born in Germany (region unknown; probably about 1840).

2. He came to California (date unknown).

3. As a young man he had been a heavy drinker and when on a spree in San Francisco, was hit and run over by a streetcar, lost a leg and wore a wooden one the rest of his life.

4. He married Mary Canesse, and they had two children: Addie (probably born in 1864 or '65) and John in 1867.

MARY MAGDALENE ("MADDIE") HATTIE DORA CANESSE HAAS PERRET

1. She was born in Alsace-Lorraine (date and place unknown; probably about 1840).

2. She came to California (date unknown).

3. She married Valentin Haas, bore him two children, eloped to Australia with John Perret in 1872, and returned to California where she bore two more sons, Bert and Frank.

4. Because her daughter's autograph album has been preserved, we know that the Perrets lived in Altamont in 1883 and 1884.

JOHN PERRET

1. He was born in Alsace-Lorraine (date and place unknown).

2. He came to California (date unknown).

3. After his elopement with Mary Canesse Haas to Australia, he returned with her to California.

4. He anglicized his surname by sounding the final *t*.

Although all three were German immigrants, there is no memory of their having spoken English with heavy accents. None was highly educated, although all were schooled in the three R's. They were Protestant. Two facts that can be safely asserted are that they all had a capacity for work and that Mary Perret had a shrewd head for business. Their industry and enterprise become more apparent after their move to Southern California in the late '80s at the height of the land boom. Whatever the passions and emotional upheavals of their earlier years, by middle age they were able to work together cooperatively and productively; although no great love was lost between Valentin Haas and John Perret, and, of course, Valentin never shared a roof with the Perrets, still, these three, with their three grown sons, became in a modest way successful in business and farming. Certainly in the late 1880s when they staked claims to land in Calabasas, they were prosperous beyond anything the Ijams had ever experienced.

Before claiming homestead land in Calabasas, Mary Perret had bought a home in Pasadena at 1441 North Los Robles Avenue. Later she was to acquire a second house on Summit Street where her son Bert lived with his second wife. She also owned and ran a small store in Pasadena and was a midwife-nurse. An indication of her forcefulness is that she is always remembered as the prime mover in the various family enterprises. It is always, "Grandma Perret did such and such," or "Grandma Perret bought such and such." The husbands seem never to be in it. She was a veritable titaness of work, of whom her granddaughter, Addie, has remarked: "I didn't know what her business was, but *she had business.*"

By 1888, the Perrets were living in Pasadena, Jack and Valentin Haas had settled in Calabasas, and Jack had gone to work at the Workman Ranch, one of the five great grain ranches owned by the Los Angeles Farm and Milling Company in the San Fernando Valley. The Perrets probably claimed their quarter sections shortly after the Haases,[35] because by the early '90s, as the letters which follow will show, there was constant travel between the two places by Mr. Perret, Jack, Bert and Frank.

Jack Haas met the Ijams family during his first year in Calabasas (how could one not meet in such a tiny settlement!), although nothing remarkable developed between the two families at first. Not only were the Haas men very busy that first year, but the Ijams took a leave of absence from Calabasas for part of 1888. At last they went, three years after the original arrangement, to Alessandro to be caretakers of their friend's property, the Ramona Hotel. But now the hotel was closed, failed because the land boom of the '80s had collapsed, leaving in its wake a depression. The interlude is chiefly remembered because of Katie. She was twelve years old, and it was the first place she had ever lived where there were carpets on the floor. They were turkey red and seemed inexpressibly luxurious and grand. In fact, the whole experience of her family having an entire hotel to live in by itself was as idyllic a memory as her earlier one of life in Santa Barbara had been. The soft life was temporary, however, and soon the Ijams returned to the rigors of Calabasas.

---

[35] John Haas' name appears (and the Perrets' does not) on a list of members in a group called Settlers' League, Calabasas, California, 1889, who had organized and retained counsel to defend their land claims in court. The days of shooting it out for a boundary line were dying. Information from Laura B. Gaye, *Land of the West Valley*, Encino, CA: Argold Press, 1975, p. 56.

Three years later, the Haas and Ijams families were not only friendly: two of their members were keeping company. Nettie, hardworking and reliable, must have seemed to John a desirable girl to cultivate as a future wife. Moreover, the Ijams' charm had probably cast its spell, their Celtic élan and high spirits plus their endless hospitality proving magnetic to one of a more inner and subdued nature. One can imagine a young bachelor living alone with his taciturn father actually falling in love with the whole family. However it worked, on Christmas, 1892, Jack Haas and Nettie Ijams announced their engagement. Two months later, she was dead.

The loss of Nettie from the close-knit Ijams family was a sorrow not easily healed. One speculates that the emotional blow Katie had sustained from her beloved sister's death manifested itself in the punishing experience she next underwent when enduring excruciating toothache, she was taken by her father in a horse and cart to Los Angeles to a dentist who gave her laughing gas, pulled all her teeth out and fitted her with false ones. She was eighteen years old.

Grief over Nettie's death and the senior Ijams' growing discontent with Calabasas were exacerbated by depression and drought. Depression they were accustomed to, but drought was a graver specter. From September, 1893, to August, 1894, there were only 6.47 inches of rain![36] The following year had a good rainfall, but in 1896 a devastating three-year drought began. Isaac E. remembered it well: the tragedy of drought—a thing man could not cope with. When stock died and what survived had to be driven out, and crops withered in the baked earth:

---

[36] Guinn, Vol. I, p. 378.

We had wells for drinking purposes, but for three years there was never enough water. The springs at Encino kept running, but not enough for a flow. People moved out. No one died from lack of water, but a lot of hopes died in those three years.[37]

Before the Ijams had settled in Calabasas, Isaac had also acquired land in Toluca on the banks of the Los Angeles River (now in Studio City). As the events of his life grew bleaker, his thoughts turned more and more to his Toluca land where, because of a better water supply, he could plant fruit orchards and Edith could be nearer her brother, Robert Shaw, who was also in that area. In the spring of 1894, he and Edith were there, and in an undated pencil-written note to her children, Edith explained why:

Dear Children:

I know you will be very much disappointed tonight, but Papa could not get through plowing, he will have today's plowing and we will be home tomorrow. We will try to come in the morning if we can possibly get there. Papa says tell Mr. Grannis if he wants to work that he can get the fencing all ready to put up, and he will be there to help him to put it up.

Now Katie dear I am sorry to disappoint you. Do not wash, unless it is a few things you need until I come.

I am nearly through planting seed, we have worked very hard to be able to go home today. Tell the boys not to get impatient, but be good.

Much love to all, Your loving mother and father

I.C. & E.C. Ijams

---

[37] Guy Fowler, "Isaac Edwin Ijams," Valley Vignettes, *The Valley Times*, October 1, 1945, page numbers missing.

Having put in their grain crop down in Toluca, the Ijams returned to Calabasas, where they grew increasingly dejected but because they were too near to claiming title to their land to be able to abandon it, they hung on through the hot dry summer months of 1894.

## The Summer of 1894

By the summer of 1894 the relationship between the Ijams and Haas-Perret families was sufficiently cultivated so that Katie and her brother Willie went to live with the Perrets in Pasadena and work in a fruit-drying business there. Having apparently surmounted her tooth difficulties of the previous year and secretly betrothed herself to John "Jack" Haas, she, at eighteen years of age, was no longer the "little woman" who had sheltered herself under her big sister's care, but was herself the womanly older daughter now in charge of her brother, Willie, sixteen.

Pasadena at that time had a population of almost 5000, and although suffering the economic aftereffects of the collapse of the real estate boom of the '80s and the devastation of its orange groves from cottony scale, it also showed signs of recuperation. Many of the plots of land that had been staked out for speculation were plowed under and groves of fruit had been planted. The Los Angeles Terminal Railroad had opened a line to Pasadena so that travel between the two towns could be accomplished easily, and the incline train up Mt. Lowe had been opened for travel in 1893.

The Ijams must have sent their children to Pasadena with easy minds, knowing its reputation for purity. The founders and early settlers of Pasadena were of a high-minded class not likely to have been frequently encountered in Calabasas.

*Mary Maddie Hattie Dora Canesse Haas Perret, born about 1840 in Alsace-Lorraine*

*Addie Haas, born in 1871*

*John Haas (Jack), born in 1867*

*Valentin Haas, born about 1840 in Germany*

# The Perret Family
## The Second Family of Mary Haas Perret

*The John Perret family, left to right: Mary Perret, Bert (behind), Frank (front), half-brothers of John Haas, and John Perret*

*The Perrets in Pasadena: John and Mary Perret, their son Bert on the porch*

*Mary Perret as an old woman at her Pasadena home on Los Robles Road, where her granddaughters Addie and Edith lived while attending Pasadena High School*

Hiram A. Reid, the town's first historian, wrote, "The first colony settlers of Pasadena were very largely of the class who keep schoolhouses and churches in the foreground wherever they go."[38] They were also "teetotal," and the same Hiram Reid, a staunch Prohibitionist, wrote a poem for the cause called "No Saloon in the Valley," of which a stanza ran:

Rise, Pasadena!
march and drill
To this your bugle's rally—
A church or school on every hill,

and NO SALOON IN THE VALLEY.[39]

No wonder Mary Perret had found her way there: if she could have invented a town for herself, it would have resembled Pasadena.

When the young Ijams came to stay with her for the summer, Mary Perret had lived in Pasadena for over five years and with her customary industry kept not only herself but everyone else on the hop. As pleasant as the change might be for the Ijams, it is doubtful that they found it as rhapsodic an experience as George Wharton James declared it to be. James, who was one of the all-time supreme boosters of Southern California and especially of Pasadena, where he made his home, once wrote:

It is a land where God smiles perpetually through a cobalt sky upon the perpetually blooming flowers where

[38] Franklin Walker, *A Literary History of Southern California*, Berkeley, CA: University of California Press, 1950, p. 156.

[39] Walker, p. 158.

children and invalids, old and young, well and weak, may alike be out-of-doors in invigorating sunshine almost very day of the year.[40]

Katie's experience of Pasadena often proved rather more mundane:

We have had very little fruit to dry this week, as the early peaches are all gone . Mrs. Perret and I have been canning fruit this week and yesterday, with the help of the boys, we did a large washing and today I ironed so consequently am feeling rather tired this eve.

Meantime, back in Calabasas, Isaac and Edith missed their children, and as the summer wore on, they wrote often, telling them the local news and Isaac often advising them in the manner of a rustic Lord Chesterfield as to the means of advancing themselves in the world. After a brief visit home by Willie, who had brought them fresh fruit for canning, Edith wrote:

Calabasas
July 21st, 1894

My dear Children,

It is now Sunday, and I will try to write you a few lines. We received Katie's letter yesterday. I would have written before now but as Willie was at home I thought he could tell you more than I could write.

I am glad you find it so plesant there for as you say it is

---

[40] James, pp. 468-69.

more than dull here. And so hot. The last few days has been up to a hundred and over.

The boys will be through thrashing this week.[41] I suppose they will not be sorry on account of the heat.

Mr. Newell stayed here last night and is here now.

I was so sorry about the fruit. I was not ready to put it up. I did not get the sealing wax until Thursday so the fruit was so ripe it will not be very good. I hope I will be able to get some more, before it is all gone. I am afraid I will not get to put up much fruit this year. I haven't got any berreys yet.

Mr. and Mrs. Grannis went to town last week.[42] Mr. Grannis was as drunk as he could be when they came home. Mrs. Grannis had to drive home. Mrs. Grannis gave me a sateen dress like yours.

Well I suppose I will have to begin on my old hobby, the chickens & turkeys, but I can finish them up as soon as the soarhead can for me, for they are all dieing again. Oh! I do feel so blue sometimes that I would like to turn my back on Calabasas forever. I have so much trouble here. My seven little guineas are all dead but three, and two of them are sick, so now I have given up the poltry business until the rains come.

Now you children stay there as long as it is plesant for you and you can make your board. I know it is so much nicer there than it is here.

I do not know what Isaac will do the balance of the

---

[41] Isaac E., Jack Haas and Frank Perret were on threshing crews at the West Ranch, one of the divisional ranches of the Los Angeles Farm and Milling Company.

[42] Probably Los Angeles

summer—perhaps go up where the horses is.

Give my kindest regards to Mr. Perret—Mrs. Perret Birt and all the others.

I believe I have nothing more to write today. I want to hear from you once or twice a week and know that you are well and I will be satisfied.

> Your loving
> mother
> E.C. Ijams

Isaac then added a page to Edith's letter:

Well Children I will add a line more to prove to you that I am mindful of you and your wellfair more than from any news of intrust I may have. It is excessively hot and the quietness of the times makes it very dull. I am glad for your sake that you are in a land of plenty and surrounded with so many pleasures and able to cancel your way.[43] Your mother keeps on the move all the time but it is so hot and dry I hardly have the ambition to struggle in the sun. However I am going to try and strike out tomorrow as I have so much in sight to do that I will have to make a beginning.

Tell Willie Mr. Kelten sent Fred back home so I have more horses than I have imployment for. The pasture where he had his have gave out, hence the cause of his sending Fred home. The boys will wind up on the West Ranch this week,[44] then I look for them home after a short rest. I do not know what they may do perhaps visit you.

---

[43] That is, pay your own way.
[44] See Note 7.

I want to haul some Straw but it is a long hot job for me.

They had a terable fight down on the ranch where the boys are at work a few days ago. One man got his nose bit off, one ear and his eye pulled out besides his cheak mutilated all about a seat at the table.[45]

Had a big Law Suit at Calabasas yesterday but it did not amount to nothing but a bill of expence. The road is lined with campers. Everybody trying to spend their time as pleasantly as possible. Be good children, give my regards to all the family.

> Your Father.

The following week Isaac wrote a note which was to be hand delivered to Katie and Willie by Jack and Frank, who had finished their threshing job, returned to their Calabasas ranches, and were on their way to their mother's in Pasadena.

> Calabasas
> July 28 1894

Dear Katie & Willie

Jack and Frank have concluded to see you today or tomorrow and I thought I would send a line of kind remembrance as they can better tell the news than I can write. Everything is quiet here—not eaven a discord

---

[45] Six weeks after this letter, the following news item appeared in the *Los Angeles Evening Express*: "Harry Bowdish, the young man charged with biting the nose of a fellow workman named Comfort, in a ranch in the San Fernando Valley several weeks ago, was given a preliminary hearing this morning by Justice Bartholomew. It was shown that Bowdish calmly and deliberately committed mayhem. He was held to answer in the sum of $500. *Los Angeles Evening Express*, August 30, 1894, front page.

which is remarkable. The censational change brings a lively shake up last night from an earthquake but no lives reported lost nor bones broaken.

The boys have wound up their harvest as they will report in person. Isaac left early this morning with the Stage to take a lode of the boys into town—

Jack and Frank have just arrived and I do not want to keep them waiting. I have no advise to give only be good children as I am proude of you. Let me remain so what time I stay with you. We are getting old and are loosing the spring from our feet which is a fore runner of the inevitable future.[46]

May God bless you and take care of you is my wish

> Resp. your
> Father &
> Mother

Three days later, the continued heat must have kept Isaac indoors and constrained him to write in this elegiac mode:

> Calabasas
> Aug the 1st
> 1894

Dear Katie and Willie

We received your note under date of July 28th last evning and was more than pleased with the contents, it bearing the good tidings of your continued good health and contented mind which is condusive to health. I am

---

[46] Isaac was to live forty-three more years.

more than glad you have so many opportunities to enjoy yourself by buggy riding and trips to the Beach, visits from kind friends who have been so long mindful of you. This is all a comfort to me and makes the otherwise lonely hours, sweet hours of meditation and satisfaction.

I have one lasting sorrow and regret to bear up under. Would to God I could have been spaired the pain —I miss Nettie so much no one but He Who gave and took her knows how all her early life clusters around my memory. Yet I have much to be greatful for. I have 3 children left who are dutiful and obedient and I am proud of them. I hope you will build yourselvs up in the estimation of your friends and newly made acquaintences.

I am proud that Mr. Hill was so mindful of you and felt such an intrust in you. I hope you will go and visit the family and continue to merit their friendship. They are good people and it is a credit to have such friends and to associate with them. It will give you confidence in yourselvs and lead you to higher spheres and callings. Places you where they are greater advantages for your future walks.

I hope you will avail yourselvs of evry opportunity to improve your society and thereby advance yourselvs morally and intellectily. I am not sighting you away from Mrs. Perret's folk. They are humble kind industrious people, worthy of example.

We are getting along all right. Time is passing rapidly. It is now the first of August a full month so you see it will soon be time for the whole brood to come home to roost. Make your time while absent both plesant and profitable. I do not anticipate you making any financial gain. If you get a few cloths and build of your social circle it will be sufficient. The boys will have visited you ere you receive this note. They can tell you more minutely the home news.

The neighborhood are all out rusteling now as a matter of course. The chief discordent element is here but has but little material to work on [47]

I got news last night that our old neighbor Mr. Douglas was dead. He died 3 or 4 days ago. One by one they go. Mrs. Penland came home yesterday but is going to return with all the kids to the Garbage field tomorrow—[48] So you see we are getting pretty well thinned out. The McCalebs have been gone all summer. The neighborhood are trying to make capital out of our school[49] but it will all die out and time will heal all discords and restore peace and harmony. I wish you a pleasent time the balance of your absence. My kind wishes to all

I.C. & E.C.

Ijams

Father &

Mother

In early August Jack returned to Calabasas briefly and then prepared to return to Pasadena where the attraction

---

[47] A reference to Harvey Branscomb and his followers. The "little material" may refer to the scarcity of stock because of their removal to other pastures on account of the drought.

[48] Editorial powers fail here. Surely not a vacation spot. A summer cleanup project perhaps?

[49] It was an unruly school and there was agitation for a male teacher. As we shall learn in the next section, one was obtained. With what results, Katie tells Jack in her letters.

of Katie's company drew him. On this trip, Isaac E. was to accompany him, and they carried with them the following letter, in which Isaac, like Shakespeare's Jaques, might have also said, "my often rumination wraps me in a most humorous sadness."

Dear Katie,

In all probability Jack will be going back to the promised land today or tomorrow and I take this opportunity to acknowledge the receipt of your last two notes which gave me so much satisfaction to know that you were not indiffrint to the council of your Father, whose whole intrusts are centered in his family and their wellfair. I have no personal aggrandizements to obtain but I have a personal intrust in my children and a desire to elevate them to comforts and spheres of usefulness.

I am not overanxious to secure them welth and ease for that does not always bring hapiness. If you could go to San Francisco New York, and other citys of welth and vanity and see the empty palaces shut up for the want of peace and harmony inside of their walls, you would then appreciate a kind home in an open board shanty but I have no need to call your attention to this feature of life.

Isaac and Jack have just come and in a hurry to go so I will close as your Mother will write you this afternoon by mail. I may add something to that. Give my kindest regards to Mrs. and Mr. Perret and share my regards with the boys. Tell Will to improve his time till the 1st of Sept. as I anticipate he will start early to school—be kind to Mrs. Perret—look after Willie's habits, and when your inclinations leads you to come home your presence will richly recompence us for the long tedious hours that has elapsed in your absence. Accept a kiss and believe me.

Your devoted
Father
I. C. Ijams

When Edith wrote, she did not concern herself with the "higher spheres and callings," but stuck to the basics of life:

Calabasas
Aug 12 / 1894

My Dear Children

It is now Sunday afternoon, & we have had our dinner, my dishes washed, now comes my promise to write, now the next question is what will I write?

Well maby you would like to know what we had for dinner, we had stewed chicking, apple sauce, tomatoes cewcumbers, bread butter & coffee. I thought Jack and Isaac would stay until after dinner so I sacrificed a chicking, had it killed and dressed, but they could not stay.

When Jack got here last night we had a jolly old crowd for supper: Newell, Henry, Fooshee and Wilmer Hartley. We had almost given Jack up, thought he was not coming. Isaac can tell you all about the lawsuit better than I can write it. One good thing, Mrs. Leffingwell has got her match in the neighborhood. Now I do not think she will want to come in contact with her very often.[50]

Papa and Isaac had a pretty hard week last week digging the cystern and hauling straw. I washed Friday had just got through and had dinner ready when they got in with there load.

Henry came with them I was putting dinner on the table who should step in but Mr. and Mrs. Bryant. Now you can emagin how I felt, wash day short dinner three extra to eat what I had cooked for three, but I made the best of it. I let them come rite along and eat what I had, and said nothing about it.

Mr. and Mrs. Bryant stayed all night, they have gone to the Conejo to hold protracted meeting, they think it will last over a week. I like Mrs. Bryant very much I think she is a very good woman. She would help me do the work all the time she was here. I think it will be grand when we get a cystern full of water the work will seem nothing then.

Eggs has come up I get 20 cts. now. I bought 20 lbs lard and will pay for it in eggs don't you think that is pretty good? Now when the boys comes home we can buy some aminition and we will live off the fat of the land quail and rabbit for a change. We have been lucky in

---

[50] Anna Leffingwell: a former dance hall entertainer from San Francisco who married a Calabasan and arrived in the area the same year as the Ijams, 1885, and was widowed thereafter. Many stories circulated about her sharp business practices, her habit of claiming her neighbors' stock should it wander over her property line and feigning of helplessness in order to manipulate others to lend her a hand. Katie remembered being occasionally "borrowed" as a child to spend the night with her when there was to be no man on her property, with instructions that if there should be any unusual sound in the night to call out "Papa! Papa!," so as to mislead any possible marauder into believing that there was a man on the premises. She is also remembered for having once poked a pitchfork into Isaac Ijams' stomach during a dispute.

getting somthing to eat. I mean in the way of fruits and vegetables. I did not can any of the peaches that Willie brought up because Papa & Isaac were hauling straw and it was so hot that we almost lived on fruit.

I do not think that any more of my chicking is taking the soar hed. They seam to have quit dying so if it does not brake out anew, I will have some left. One out of the four little guineas died.

You must all take observations about drying fruit. It will be useful to you some time.

You boys must not forget that bill for the Youths Companion. If I had any money I wold pay part of it

You wanted to know how I put in my time. I manage to get it in some way so it does not seem so very long. I am trying to make my dress Mrs. Grannis gave me. I have the waist all done but the sleeves. I don't know where to find the sleeve pattern I will take a good look for it tomorrow.

When you all come home I think I will go to your uncles for a few days.[51] They sent me up some lovely tomatoes yesterday.

Well it is getting time for me to tend to the chickings, now you must all write three letters for my one, for there will be three of you to write.

> From your
> loving mother,
> E. C. Ijams

---

[51] Robert Shaw, near Toluca.

If Isaac did nothing else in the summer of 1894, he wrote letters. Although most in this book were composed on Sunday, the one which follows was written on Monday. It was hot and instead of struggling in the sun Isaac chose to remain indoors and pen this lengthy account of village events to his absent children. Among the various topics discussed are the upcoming Republican Primary Election and Isaac's call to Jack to be home for it.

To unravel the political ins and outs of Calabasas in the '90s would require a full dissertation. What is necessary to understand is that the bounty system prevailed: whichever political party was in power had the privilege of dispensing jobs and sinecures to its partisans. There was not much bounty in Calabasas, but what there was of it was hungrily sought by both sides. Electioneering was, therefore, an engrossing activity as the day of choice approached. For the Ijams and their friends, there was always the hope that Harvey A. Branscomb and his forces would be bested. Much depended on who worked on the election board as vote-influencing was flagrant at the polls. An article in the *Los Angeles Evening Express* contrasted two polling places in Los Angeles: one, held in the open air under a pepper tree where everything is "pleasant, cool and good-natured," and another, having trouble with one "Sutherland and his ringsters," had rallied the law-abiding forces under the battle cry: "Marshal up our forces and we'll try to win our part of the pudding."[52]

Isaac E. liked to tell of a time when a rearranged election board in Calabasas prevented Harvey A. Branscomb from winning his part of the pudding:

---

[52] *Los Angeles Evening Express,* August 30, 1894, p. 3.

73

My father and the other settlers had decided to throw Harvey out. They chose Daly Nash to run against him. Charley Bell, the son of Major Horace Bell was on the election board and he favored Branscomb. He could speak Spanish and if he sat on the board we knew he could influence the Mexican vote.

Well, my father went to see Major Bell and explained the situation. The major listened and said: 'I'll remonstrate with Charley, sir, I'll remonstrate with him.'

On election day, they chose me to sit on the board if Charley failed to show up. You see, I could speak Spanish, too. Branscomb lost by four votes and contested the election in the Los Angeles court. The late Earl Rogers, who later became District Attorney, represented Branscomb, but lost the case.

Branscomb later met Charley Bell in a saloon and wanted to know why he hadn't shown up with the election board.

Now Charley used to drive a mule to a buckboard.

I guess he didn't want to say anything about the old Major Bell remonstrating with him. So he said to Branscomb:

'This mule of mine got drunk that night, Harvey—and I had to sleep out there in a ditch.'[53]

---

[53] Oral humour doesn't travel well to the printed page, so you'll have to take my word for it that when Isaac E. (by then called Uncle Ike) told this story to family gatherings and came to the line, "I'll remonstrate with Charley, etc.", he brought down the house. Uncle Ike was a deadpan humorist of the frontier tradition. I can only pay tribute to his gift for timing. I cannot resurrect the fun and laughter.

Dear Children

I will make a joint stock of all the news I have in store.
You can divide with Jack and Bert. Hence there will be
no secrets. I am just in receipt of Katies note containing
the sad news of the death of poor old Jack whose alloted
time was so well improved, peace to his ashes. I hope it
will not be the fate of any more as I am looking forward
to speedy deliverence from threatening starvation for
the poor animals. September is near at hand and that is
boardering on a rainy mon.

It is very hot and quiet here now. There is nothing
prospering but irons.[54] They have been doing well recently.
Mr. H. A. Branscomb the high official and Government
post master of Calabasas[55] got into a difficulty with his
Brother Ben Friday evning, and I understand that fire
arms were brought into use but no serious accident. I saw
Harve today and see some of the beautiful complection
was torn off of his cheak and the other was a deep crimson
from the use of intoxicating fluids.

Next comes Lefingwell with her atty and says that one
Mrs. Bently did unlawfully seize and carry away 7 sacks
of wheat earned by her hard toil and paid for with one of
her neighbors turkeys in good faith. But Mrs. Bently met
the alegation with her wise counsel whose knowledge and
wisdom was sufficient for the emergency. After a short
shuffel he gave the honorable cort to understand that Mrs.

---

[54] Guns.

[55] It must have galled the Ijams to have lost the post office to Branscomb.

Lefingwell had again given them a missdeal—And again Mrs Bently was allowed to go in peace about her daily avocations. Lefingwell has retired from the Turf.

There is nothing exciting in the immediate neighborhood. There is considerable electioneering going on and I have to meet the diffrent issues in diffrent lights. I want Jack to undergo a little drill when he comes home. He will realise that Truth is stranger than fixion. I keep pretty close up to the changes but I want him here a short time before the primarys which comes off on the 28th. Tell him to write me so I will know how to Ledge[56] but it will be necessary to our mutual intrust that he be here at the primarys of the Republicans

*Here Isaac gives names of men to trust and not to trust in the coming election. No surnames; only given names: meaningless today*

I am going to Mr. Shaws in the morning to get a load of tomatoes to peddle.[57] He has a lot ripe and spoiling and the cannery will not open till the 1st of Sept. Hence the necessity of retailing them out.

I may load with kids the first time as they have a surplus on hand. They fell air to a new one a few days ago. A Mrs. Ackerman, one of old man Hills from Chatsworth daughter, had started to the Beach for a time and got to the Shaws place, and camped. In the night coming events began to cast their shadows around them, accompanied by severe pains and they knocked at the dore for admittince and council, which resulted in Ella Mitchell proffering her bed to the comfort of the Stranger, and Eddie struck out

---

[56] Keep a tally or a ledger at the polls.

[57] See Index, Shaw and Mitchell, for this and the paragraph which follows.

for medical aid. Sister Mary Stormed around and changed the roosting place of all the family. In the meanwhile Mrs. Ackerman formerly Mrs. Hunter fooled them all by not waiting on any of them. In less time than I have been penning the event she rewarded the entire party—by giving birth to a young kid—

While the devoted father is a light brunett with light hair, the condition of his feelings made his skin look like it was off of the same place, Viz: white. The loving mother is of a sandy complection and a decendent of a redheaded Father yet with all these facts the ofspring has a remarkable heavy sut of black hair while the remainder of its physical fraim is covered with a heavy coating of dark skin. The eyes are in harmony; hence the room for a dispute as to ownership but as long as there is no question raised, all will be sunshine.

I hope you will all have a good enjoyable time and make enough to pay your board and be sure and do it as long as you enjoy yourselves so do we in the knowledge that you are all well and happy. We miss you 23 hours out of 24, yet we can reconcile ourselves when we know that you are well and surrounded by comforts and friends. I shall anticipate Willie home by the 10th of Sept as that is when school opens unless he is earning enough to justify him in remaining out of school longer. Your mother is canning Tomatoes. Our fruit is ripening in the home orchard. I think Coxys industrial Army will be along in time to help us to pick it and save the heaviest portion as the Linnets are busy helping.

Resp.

I. C. Ijams

Isaac's reference to Coxey's Army is ironic but serves to remind that 1894 was a year characterized by strikes and riots throughout the nation. In July, President Cleveland had sent in troops against the workers in the great Pullman strike, and the word scab became current to describe a strike-breaker. General Jacob Sechier Coxey led a throng of unemployed workmen eastward to Washington with a demand for issue of $50,000,000 in paper money and public works for the unemployed. Coxey and some of his attendants were arrested in March, 1894, for walking on the grass with the intent to commit a demonstration below the capitol.[58] Known as the Army of the Commonweal, it had attracted men from Oregon and California who had been discharged from halted railroad work, and there had been outbreaks of violence between Commonwealers and sheriffs in the two states.

All this strife must have seemed remote to the homesteading Calabasans, however—subject for a little joke in a letter. Thomas Beer, the historian, once described the rural American of the 1890s as "a colonist, within his own country,"[59] which aptly describes the Calabasas folk, whose vital concerns centered around survival in a drought year. Isaac, as we shall see in the following letter, was casting about for a way to leave Calabasas, which is why he wanted Katie and Isaac to search out the property of a Mr. Picket in Pasadena for a possible rental. There was a great deal of bartering, trading and renting of land at that time, and Isaac apparently had in mind to keep his Calabasas land (hence

[58] Irving S. and Nell M. Kull, *A Short Chronology of American History: 1492-1950*, Brunswick, N.J., Rutgers University Press, 1952. p. 182.

[59] Thomas Beer, "Hanna," *Hanna Crane and the Mauve Decade*, New York, Alfred A. Knopf, 1941. p. 486.

the need for a fence so that no one could trespass and make a pre-emptive claim) and rent elsewhere until the drought was over.

Calabasas

Sept the 3 1894

Dear Children

Time is rapidly passing away ladened with care and responsibility. The boys got home with the horses in poor shape for winter storms, but it was the best they could do. I hardly know what to do with them till feed comes. I wish I could scatter them around to earn their own feed. Jack is hauling straw intending to keep his home. I would like very much to see you at home but if you are making a dollar you had better nurse your job a while longer. We can in all probability anticipate rain in October. If we can get through till grass comes perhaps we can then wipe out and commence anew.

I calculate to move the family away from here as soon as we can get a title and we will want a good fence around the place. Katie if you could find out where Mr. Pickets property is in Pasadena and you and Isaac could look at it and see if it would soot you and your mother—if so it might soot to rent it especially if it has to be looked after at any expence. You might find out by corresponding with some of your relitives.

I am tired of Calabasas. We had a great time at the Primary election. Evry body got drunk and have remained so—

The rest of this letter is missing, so we have no way of

79

knowing if Isaac reported that the Branscomb forces had enjoyed a victory at the polls, but Edith in a later letter wistfully remarked, "I have become indifferent to who is elected."

The day before Isaac wrote his melancholy lines, another unhappy Calabasan, Jack Haas, wrote a loving intimate letter to Katie to whom he had now been secretly engaged for seven months. That Jack and Katie should have been drawn to each other after Nettie's death is not surprising. Bonds of affection and closeness had already existed between the two. "My best regards to Mr. Haas or I mean Jack," Katie had saucily written to Nettie in the summer of 1892 when she was sixteen and Nettie about to depart for Ventura. Nettie's "When you see Jack I guess he will have something to tell you" suggests that it was Jack himself who told Katie that he and Nettie were to be engaged. She had been the little sister and confidante of the older pair, the third member of a loving trio. With Nettie gone they had sought consolation in each other's company and fallen in love.

Calabasas

Sept 2n 1894

My dearest Katie

I hardly know what to write now since I have started. News there is none. And never will be in this forsaken place. Darling I never was as tired of a place in my life as I am this, at present.

A person hears of nothing but quarrels continually. And the hills look so dry—and barren.

This has been a lonely week for me I assure you. The

only thing that has been pleasant for me is thoughts of you. Dear I never felt the need of a dear one as much as I do now. If it were not for you Katie, I am sure I would not be able to stand the discouragement.

Your Father was down here this morning.[60] And I went over to Mr. Gates with him. Your father and Leon Gates had a quarrel yesterday. And he abused your dad. Shamefully. I wan't present but Mr. Fooshee told me. And he said he never heard such language as that boy used. Mr. Gates went up to try and get him to come home, and if he don't, your father is going to have him arrested. And try and send him to the reform school. He should have caught the kid and beat him to death. Of course you know the instigation of it. H.A.B.[61] He is the one that ought to be punished. Your Father would be justified in shooting that wretch in my opinion. And I am sure were I in his place I would not stand any more of his abuse. But I will not say anything for he knows best. He is older than me and has had more experience.

I had a caller myself last night just after I went to bed. Manuel Booth passed along the road, and he called me and said there was a woman down the road that wanted some help as her horse had given out. I dressed and went down. And who should it be but Mrs. Leffingwell.[62] And she was a great-looking outfit, I assure you. She had led the old horse as far as she could and now she was stuck for good. So I had to help the old woman—as much as I hated to.

---

[60] It was Sunday.

[61] Harvey A. Branscomb.

[62] See Note 16, this section.

Katie I have just upset the ink bottle. Fortunately I did not get any on the letter, but on everything else on the ranch, I think. A great looking mess here just now.

I suppose Bert and Joe arrived home safe. I was down to the ranch and saw Frank last week.[63] He was drying fruit—but I think he was eating more than anything else.

Your Mother has been canning some peaches this last week that she got from Mr. Hill of Chatsworth. School is to commence here tomorrow a week—unless the teacher gets here sooner. Jas Penland's folk are still absent.

I will postpone till after I do the chores. Then I will spend the eve with you.

Part 2nd

After Chore Time. And good bed Time for a lazy man.

Well Darling. I suppose you have put in a hard week in Pas. How much longer will you be drying fruit yet, do you think. Maybe I will get a chance to come down and help you out before you get through. I stopped and had dinner with Aunt Mary and Uncle Robert as I came out and visited with them for some time. And I had a pleasant time. Tot was full of fun, though she was complaining of a cold. Mary came out to your place with me. So you see I had a pleasant trip out here after all—but it was awful warm—And that is all. Frank & Dad are asleep—and that is where I ought to be.

I wish I could kiss you good night—just once, darling.

---

[63] Jack's half-brother, Frank Perret, seems to have been the steadiest worker at the Perret ranch, and he became a permanent settler. Bert, the other half-brother, came and went, eventually settling in Pasadena near his mother.

How that would satisfy my longings words cannot express. But I ought to be glad I am alive in place of wishing for such luxuries—

Hopeing you will not be as mean as I was and make me wait a whole week for an answer, for I shall look for one about the middle of the week.

With best wishes and fondest love I remain ever yours,

Jack

excuse mistakes

Good Night Darling Happy Dreams

Darling for my sake won't you Katie.   I know you will. By by.


Katie answered promptly:


Pasadena

Sep. 7, 1894

My Dear Jack,

At last I find a few minutes time in which to answer your kind letter and tell you how much I appreciated it, although it seemed a long time in coming.

But to know that you still find time to think of me, and pleasure in doing so, is a great consolation and makes amends for what would otherwise have been a rather long week.

Although the boys are still here and everyone is kind, I do miss you sorely, dear Jack. When I read your letters from home it makes my heart ache, for I know how lonely and quiet it must be there. It makes me wish all the more to be there and help to bear my share of the burden.

Do not be discouraged dearest. They say "all things come to those that wait," so surely our turn will come soon.

We have had very little fruit to dry this week, as the early peaches are all gone. There were a few pears come in, which Mrs. Boughrider cut and that is about all that has been done in the drier this week.

Your mother and I have been canning fruit this week and yesterday, with the help of the boys, we did a large washing and today I ironed so consequently am feeling rather tired and sleepy this eve.

The boys are away this evening. They have gone to some political meeting. They have become entheusastic poloticians. Bert and Max have been giving us stump speaches all day.

They have been employing themselves the last few days by painting Bert's cart.

Your mother has taken in another girl much younger than I. Perhaps you know an old widower by the name of Meyers. He came here last Sunday and staid all night with his three little children. The little girl wanted to stay so your mother is keeping her. Such a chatterbox! She is sitting by my side talking to your mother and it is a wonder I can collect my wits at all.

You asked how all the boys and girls are. As far as I know they are all well. Max is in good spirits and as dull as ever.

I have seen none of the girls this week, except Lady Flint. I know she is the one you would have asked for had you been brave enough. She tells your mother that she thinks you boys "just about right," as bro. Frank would express it.

I am sorry Papa and Leon had trouble. I was so in hopes Papa could shear clear of any more rows for a while at least. But I fear he never will in that place.

I can imagine how you enjoyed getting up out of bed to help Mrs. Leffingwell. You did better by her than I could. I think I should have felt inclined to help her over the embankment.

Well My Dear Boy I fear you will find my letters something like I am—uninteresting. But believe me Jack I am not half the hard hearted creature that I seem. I do love you truely and sincerely but have not the way to show my appreciation for all your goodness to me. I often feel unworthy of your love when I think of all you have done for me and how little I can do in return. But you will have to wait for that. Maybe some day I can 'pay you off.' You must write sooner next time if you expect me to get you an answer by the middle of the week. I only rec'd yours day before yesterday, and that with my own hands.

Good night dear Jack. Count every mistake and blot as a kiss and I know you will have enough such as they are for once. With fondest love, I am

Your own

Katie

*At the top of the second sheet*

It is ten o'clock and you can see by the last page of my letter that I am sleepy. Remember me to bro. F. and write soon for it lightens my spirits wonderfully. Do come as soon as you can. We will be thru as soon as we finish late peaches.

Yours.

In mid-September, Willie returned to Calabasas to begin school while Katie and Isaac E. remained in Pasadena to work at fruit drying. Isaac wrote Katie one more letter in which there was no mention of his altercation with the Gates boy, but he continued his instructions to investigate Mr. Picket's property in Pasadena. Ultimately, this came to nothing, and the Ijams were to remain in Calabasas for several more years.

Calabasas

Sept. 14 1894

Dear Little Kittie

While Willie is answering a nice kind letter that he received from his Brother Isaac I will acknowledge the receipt of yours under a more recent date. While it is a satisfaction to receive a note from you it would be much more enjoyable to have a social interview with you face to face, but all things considered perhaps it is better to wait till you will not have to place a limit on your time to remain at home. It looks like you had been favored in getting such pleasant surroundings this summer.

As long as you are unfortunate enough to have to accept from some advantages to help yourself to comforts, Mrs. Perret is instructive moral and a business woman—all desireable qualities and indeed I feel greatful for what they have done for the family especially yourself. Remember me in the kindest terms you can to Mrs. P. It has given you an insight to business.

I am glad you have apparantly regained your health. I hope you will continue to improve in health and usefulness. In my fancy it will not be long till the winter winds will begin to howl, and then you will need to be robust to tide over till Spring.[64]

This neighborhood remains Statu Co, that means 'unchangeable, the same.'

In speaking of Mr. Picket's property your mother says his name is John Picket. She does not know that he has a middle innitial but she has an old friend in Pasadena that went to school with her in Lousiana by the name of Wm C Hendrix. He is running a Dairy there or was 2 years ago. He is well acquainted with Mr. Picket and your mother thinks he would know all about his property. You can easily hunt him up.

Burt can get on to him in a little while. I found out his occupation on the Great Register that was 2 year ago this fall. He may have changed his business. Find out all you can that will be of intrust in the future and when you come home we will plan our future.[65]

I was at your Aunt Mary's on Tots birthday. They spoke very kindly of you, wishing you were there but I do not believe any one wanted you and Isaac there as bad as I did. I think had you of been there, there would have been

---

[64] Isaac must have had his fears that Katie might suffer Nettie's fate. The trauma of the tooth pulling doubtless weakened her and may account for her poor health in the spring of '94.

[65] It was to be Calabasas.

no trouble in picking out the bell of the evning, although Tot assumed, but lacked the culture and dignity.

Share this note with Isaac and tell him I will look forward with pleasure to the time of his return home. I will go and help his uncle when he comes back.

Tell Max that I think your Uncle Robert will be glad to give him a job picking tomatos when he gets done the fruit deal. So will he Isaac.

With kind wishes to everybody I remain your affectionate

Father

At the end of summer, Katie lingered on in Pasadena, and as this last letter from her mother indicates, Jack had joined her to spend a little pleasant time in her company before returning to the hard times in Calabasas where the drought and depression were taking their toll.

Calabasas
Sept. 23rd 1894

Dear Katie

I have not forgotten you if I haven't writen to you for two weeks. When I herd the boys had come away I did not know but what they were through with the fruit and you too would come home until Willie got your letter day before yesterday.

Willie and I are alone. Papa has been at your Uncle's since last Monday, helping with the beans. He is working to get the bean hay to help pull the horses through. The horses are looking pretty bad. Mike Stroser fetched one of Jacks and Willies mares home yesterday. Willie took Jack's home this morning. He has not got back yet. Mr. Beckwith said this morning that one of Jack's cows was sick. He said he thought she was poisoned and would die.

It is very hot here again for the last week, but I hope we will have a change soon.

Mrs. Branscomb did not stay long only two or three days. I did not see her. I herd she come after Dick but she did not get him.[66] I understand she is now at Bessie Settles. Beckwith told me that there were some papers at Jack's for him to serve.[67] I believe Mrs. Leffingwell is after Branscomb, but I suppose he will be home before you get this letter.

The peoples party[68] nominated Richerdson Branscomb Brown & Nash. There was no one there to take the part of the other side so they had it there own way. I have become indiferent to who is elected. The sooner the people runs there corse in this neighborhood the better I will like it. I am only praying that I may be able to spend a few peaceful days of my life somewhere else.

It is too bad the price of dryed fruit is so low. Will Johnson told me he took some dryed peaches to town last week and could only get 5 cts. a lb. He is peddling his mother's fruit now. He says it is hard to sell it as there is no money in the Country.

Willie has just got home, Jack's cow died. Mr. Beckwith thinks it is the water. Frank fetched home a little Jersey

---

[66] Her son.

[67] Jack Haas was a deputy sheriff in Calabasas.

[68] The Populist Party, largely agrarian, was strongly in favor of Free Silver.

cow with a young calf last week.

Willie says to tell Jack that his folks want him to hurry up and get out here.[69]

You never said whether you got my last letter or not, or your papa's.

Well I believe I have writen all that I can think of. Take good care of yourself and be a good girl. I would like to see you but I do not want to hurry you home now for there is nothing pleasant to invite you to.

Kindest regards to Mrs. Perret and all the family.

Hoping you will continue to have a good time.

I am as ever,

Your loving mother,

E. C. Ijams

As the summer of 1894 ended, all thoughts and prayers were for rain and at the end of September a little fell (00.73 inch), but it proved a false harbinger as October and November remained dry.

## The Long Engagement

When the fruit harvest was over in Pasadena, Katie returned to her home in Calabasas to hear "the winter winds howl." Jack shared his time between the two places and although the engaged couple was able to spend some time together in Calabasas and attend a few dances in the

---

[69] That would be his father, Valentin, and brother Frank. Evidently Jack was overstaying his leave.

*John Haas and Katie Ijams became secretly engaged on February 24, 1894*

autumn, as Christmas approached they were separated and the following correspondence took place. They wrote as all lovers do when apart, distance itself lending them the courage to make protestations of love and revelations of feeling which would not have been so easy had they been face to face. They are endearing letters, but what gives them their special flavor and interest are the accounts of their activities and the brief scenes of life in Pasadena and Calabasas.

The first letter from Jack includes an invitation to Katie to spend the holidays with his family in Pasadena. Mary Perret certainly must have been wise to the romance that was flourishing between the two young ones, even though they kept their intention to marry a secret. The continued secrecy of their engagement long after the traditional twelve-month mourning period for Nettie had passed must have been prompted in part by fear of scandal in Calabasas. The delay of their marriage is understandable for economic reasons: depression, drought and the uncertainty of Jack's plans (he debates in his letter of January 13th whether to leave Calabasas and move to Pasadena in order to improve his lot), but this does not explain their reticence about announcing their betrothal. Jack and Katie were not given to subtle introspection nor were they nonconformists. Respectability and a proper appearance were important to them, and the propriety of their marrying must have been an issue, because the ancient taboos surrounding the choice of a marriage partner pull like a powerful and often unacknowledged undertow, even in the relaxed social atmosphere of a frontier settlement.[70] Not wishing to be talked about and knowing how gossip thrived in Calabasas for lack of other recreation, the couple chose discretion and silence.

Then there was the question of Isaac Ijams' opinion. His blessing was important to them. What will Papa think? had certainly crossed Katie's mind as her romance with Jack had developed, and older wiser Jack must have given

---

[70] Katie and Jack were the unconscious inheritors of two ancient and contradictory traditions: one derived from the Bible, the other from British and Northern European custom and law. The law of the Old Testament ordered that a brother take to wife the widow of his own brother in order to preserve the family (called the levirate marriage, Deuteronomy, xxv, 5-10, its classic example is the marriage of Boaz to Ruth). On the other hand, until 1907 when the law was abolished, a widower in England was forbidden to marry his deceased wife's sister. Under the Laws of Marriage in the Church of England's *Book of Common Prayer*, such a union was forbidden, although a marriage of first cousins was acceptable. In the 1850's, an Englishman, Henry Thornton, a member of Parliament, attempted to have the law changed when he wished to marry his deceased wife's sister. He failed, and his marriage to his sister-in-law resulted in their exile to France, the loss of his ancestral estate and a great scandal and humiliation to his family (see *Marianne Thornton*, by E.M. Forster, NY, Harcourt, Brace and Co., 1956). As late as 1956 in England, a widow was still impeded from marrying her deceased husband's brother.

the matter some thought also. Proud Isaac, who wrote to Katie that had she been at her cousin Tot's birthday party, she would have been "the bell of the evening, although Tot assumed, but lacked the culture and dignity;" Isaac, who urged his daughter to "improve your society and thereby advance yourself morally and intellectily," adding, "I am not sighting you away from Mrs. Perret's folk. They are humble kind industrious people;" Isaac may have aspired higher than the Haases and Perrets for his Katie. "Humble kind industrious" were all very well, but for a man who had his sights raised to "the higher spheres and callings," the terms did not constitute an ultimate accolade.

As the letters will show, all Katie's doubts had been resolved, and she was eager for marriage. Almost nineteen and trapped in an environment which offered her almost no pleasant options except marriage, she was at a loose end, like an idle actress between engagements—no longer Papa's girl and not yet Jack's wife. When Jack's letter, written shortly before Christmas, arrived with its invitation to spend part of the holidays with him in Pasadena, she must have been delighted.

Pasadena, Cal.

Dec. 16th 1894

My own Darling—

You will no doubt be disappointed Tuesday eve, when you get to your Uncle's to find no Jack in sight. But Katie it is impossible for me to get there as my time will be all taken up here at home.[71]

---

[71] Apparently a pre-Christmas family party at the Shaws in Toluca.

But I hope you will have a pleasant time just the same, for I know your Aunt will make it as pleasant as possible for you. And I would like very well for her sake to be there.

I was in L.A. yesterday after a load of hay and will go there again tomorrow. And then I have some work to do here at home—so I cannot tell when I can get out to Calab.

But Darling if it were not for you, I would not care much when it was. Believe me jewel it is harder for me to be parted from you than Pen can describe. This has been one of the loneliest days I have spent in sometime. How I longed for your company today. If I could but have folded you in my arms and gotten one of those loveing kisses you have in store for me. But Honey it seems our lot is a hard one just at present. And I do hope the day is not far distant when we can enjoy each others company continually for I know it will be a happy one.

Mother said she expected you would come down with me this trip. I don't know what could have put that into her head for I never said a word about you coming.

Well Darling: Everybody is in bed but me and I ought to be there. I have your old bedroom now. And I never enter without thinking of its former occupant. And how I wish she was there tonight.

Katie write me when you get home from the sociable— and tell me all the news. And don't forget about coming down if you can.

> With best wishes
> and fondest love,
> I remain Your
> Jack

94

*back page*

I wish dear you could spend the Hollidays with us here in Pas. Mother says you must come N. Years Day if you cant before, for they are going to have a big time here. A Tournament of Roses that has never been equalled. And races, and I know not what all. So Katie if possible come. I will come up and get you if you can come. And I think your folks ought to let you have a little while off anyway.

I will be pretty lonesome here about that time, for I expect Mother and I will be alone—for Bert will be at the Raymond[72] as they open on the 22nd. So come. Be sure to come. Come anyway.


That Katie did get to Pasadena for part of the holiday is revealed in this next letter from Jack.

Pasadena

Jan 13th 1895

Dearest Katie—

I expected to be with you before this when I left Cala. But circumstances allways alters cases. When I got home, Mr. Perret was ready to go out next day—so that left me here to do the few odd jobs.

I am going to do some hauling for Mr. Singer next week. I don't know how long it will take me perhaps all week. Then if nothing else turns up I will come out. I was to Los Angeles Friday—And got the Appointment as Dept.

---

[72] See page 106.

Sheriff. So if I behave I will have a star for the next four years anyway.

Darling I suppose this day has been as lonely to you as it has been to me. I have been home this whole day reading when I could collect my wits enough. There is nothing new or strange happened here since you left. Bert is still working at the well. I was down yesterday for the first time to see it. It sure is a great well. They have a stream of water as large as a stove pipe running from it all the time.

Bert's girl is back on the Island teaching again, so he is no better off than I am.[73] All by his lonesome. She had her picture taken while in town and he expected to get one today. Bert has just got home, and I expect I will get a glimpse of that aforesaid photo.

Mother is about the same as usual. Up one day—and down the next. I hope your mother has found something that helped her arm ere this.

I have asked Mr. Mundell if he wanted to trade his town property for a ranch. At least Mother did—He said he did and would come out and look at it. But Katie I hardly know which I like best. Town, or the ranch. While you are here it seems I like Town the best but when alone I am as disatisfied as I can be, so I am thinking that it is not much difference where a person is if they are separated from the one they love—they cannot be satisfied. So I don't care so much if I trade or not. But if I can get what I want I will trade.

Your father wanted me to speak to Cheesebrough if I met

---

73  Dolly, who became Bert's first wife, taught school at Avalon, Catalina Island.

him but I did not. And I did not have time to go and see
him. I went to the School Sup. Office as he requested. But
they had already employed a teacher and he intended to
go out with McCaleb the next day, so I suppose you have
school by this time. . .

The rest of this letter is lost, but the story of the teacher
continues with the following undated fragment of a letter
obviously written by Katie at this same time:

alone, during all the rain, with the exception of a new
and valued member of the family, viz: a Swan. I don't
suppose you have ever heard of such a thing, but tis so.
Tis not one of your long-necked, white plumed swans, but
a living, walking talking Swan. Sent out by the County
Supt. of Schools. There you know it all. Aren't you afraid
your best girl is in danger, living in the same house with
a very intelligent, I mean, unintellegant, young man. You
need not be, dearest, you have intrusted your heart in safe
keeping and it is only my desire to tease that prompts
me to write such stuff.

I have waisted most two sheets of good paper to write
nothing but mere foolishness but I want to make it (my
letter) so long that you will be ashamed of your little note,
as sweet as it was. You said you didn't know anything
new to write. I don't want to hear anything new. Tell me
the Same Old Story. I love it best. Just write over & over
I love you Katie, and just see how pretty it looks.

But there dear I really am silly tonight and if I keep
writing at this rate, I'll not be able to get my letter in an
ordinary envelope. So I am going to postpone untill in the

morning. There, don't kick! You'll get it just as soon.

This leaves me sitting in the dining room listening to the rain which has begun to fall again in torrents. Good night dear heart and pleasant dreams—

Katie was right. The rain did fall in January, 1895. The drought had been broken in the previous December with over four and a half inches of rain. Then in January almost six inches came down. It was a cause for celebration and anecdotes.

Pasadena

Jan. 24th, 1895

Dearest Katie—

I will try to do as you asked me to, in your sweet letter. Tell you the old—old story. Tell you how your image is before me continually.

Darling I wish I was with you this eve, for I could tell you far better how I love you than I can write it.

Well Honey, I am not much surprised by the arrival of a Swan in your family circle for this is the time of year to expect them. I hope he makes it pleasant for you. O, how I envy him his boarding place. I am sure I would keep you busy looking after my wants.

You spoke of some rain in your letter—Well I should smile—It commenced raining here one Sunday night and never quit untill the next Sat. one continual downpour. We hardly got out of the house all week. But Bert and I caught fits Sunday. Bill Stewart got out of Grub, and could not get any of the grocery men to take him up what he

wanted oweing to the high water in the creek. So we had
to see that Nell did not go hungry. And she had a picnic.
But I got off the best. Bert and Bill had rubber boots.
And I had none so they had to do all the packing and the
stream ran so swift they could hardly stand up in it. It
was as good as a circus to see them reeling around in the
water up to the top of their boots. But they got there all
the same and then Nell treated us to a fine dinner. While
we were eating—the kids upset the pots that were on
the stove and there was a mess—Stew, Kids and what
not in a pile.

We are haveing lovely weather here at present. And the
Mts. look fine when the sun shines on them. They have
been covered with snow for some time. The snow was
below the Mt. Lowe hotel. The Tenderfeet are more than
going to the Mts. now, to see the snow. It seems homelike
to them I suppose.

Mother was downtown this afternoon and brought home
a large lamp—it is about as big as your warming stove.
And I have had more fun with her than you can shake
a stick at about it. I tell her that she did not get it all, as
there is a cart goes with it—To move it about.

The rest of the letter is lost, but we have part of Katie's
reply to it, which she wrote on a Sunday morning:

I shall miss you very much today, it does not seem like
Sunday unless I get a glimpse of you. Last S—I put in
very plesantly. Frank & Isaac were up and after dinner
we went for a strole over the hills. I felt rather lonely
after they left, but consoled myself with talking with
Mr. Swan.

Isaac came up this morning. He says they are liable to be turned off tomorrow.[74]

I haven't heard from our place,[75] but don't think any of the hills have washed away.

Do just as you please about trading your place. You know whatever you do pleases me. I can be happy anywhere with you.

Remember me to your mother and Bert. I am so sorry your mother's health does not improve. Mamma too is not well. She suffers continually with her arm besides numerious other complaints.

You will have to come and see me now, dear. We have taken the teacher to board and I'll not be able to get away for a long time.[76]

I had to have something to do to keep from being miserable.

I know of nothing more of interest, so will close for this time, hoping and expecting to hear from you very soon. I send my best love and a kiss and that is more than you did.

> Your ever
> loving
> Katie

P.S. I am very glad you do not have to give up that pretty silver star. Be a dear good boy and keep it.

---

[74] Whatever ranch he was working for was probably laying off men because of the rain.

[75] That is, the Haas ranch.

[76] Edith Ijams was now 56 years old with one arm crippled by either bursitis or arthritis. She probably could not have managed the extra work of keeping a boarder without Katie.

Another undated fragment of a letter from Jack written during this same period:

I suppose the new teacher entertains you of evenings. I hope it is not so lonesome for you now, as you have something to keep you imployed.

You ask in your letter if I am not afraid of my best girl living in the same house with a very inteligent young man. I am glad you have such company. And Jewell I love you too dearly, and know you would do nothing out of my sight but what is perfectly right.

I have not been doing much the last couple of days but go to work again in the morning. Mr. Singer sold his place here on the hill. To a Mr. Hunt. Hope he improves it. Things will look better around here then.

When is your Uncle going to the mines? Is your Pa going along?[77]

*Here follows a series of instructions about papers from the Los Angeles County Sheriff's Office which he asks her to attend to, adding the remark, "Haven't I got plenty of cheek."*

I suppose the grass is fine on the hills now. And the poor stock are picking up. You write that you have not heard from our ranch. I think you had better keep posted. Bert will tell you everything was all right when I last heard from there, so your mind will rest easy.

---

[77] Gold fever still burned in Isaac Ijams and his brother-in-law, Robert Shaw. They had a claim at Randsburg, California, on the Mojave Desert along the county lines of Kern and San Bernardino.

Darling I wish I could kiss you good night. And be able to tell you how I love—love—love—love you. When I come up I expect to have plenty of sweet kisses waiting for me—And get a peep into your loving eyes—and be asked as usual, What are you looking at? Honey, Good night. With kisses and love

                                        from your Jack

Write me soon darling. You done fine last time.

                              Calabasas,
                              Calif.

Jan. 30, 1895

Dearest Jack:

I was so glad to receive your letter yesterday. It seemed like an age since I had heard from you, although it really wan't so long. It takes quite a while for your letters to get here. The last one was dated the 24th and I never got it until yesterday, the 29th. Almost a week getting these few miles.

I was in hopes to see you before now. If I could just get such a dear letter every day as I received yesterday I would try to be satisfied. I try to be as it is, but it is hard to do. I fear I have not learned that one thing that we all have to know to be happy, and that is to be content with my lot.

We have had quite a seige of company this week. Aunt and Flora made us quite a visit, also Roscoe Overman.

Flora made a great mash on the Teacher. She told Roscoe that was what she came up for and I believe it. She and Mr. Swan sat in this big cold room and talked until 11 o'clock.

While the rest of us sat by the stove and played cards. He (Mr. Swan) is the biggest failure I ever saw, out of school, and they say he is as bad in it. You need never fear of me falling in love with him, even if you had no confidence in me whatever.

His wisdom is about as short as the trousers he wears and they strike him just below the knees.

He is too contrary and to fond of argueing to be a plesant companion. I too wish you had his boarding place. I would devote my time trying to please you, Dearest.

It makes me very happy to have you trust me so completely. God grant that you may never have cause to do otherwise.

The boys expect to be through today or tomorrow, at least Isaac does. I don't know whether Frank does or not.

Papa and Willie are sowing grain and plowing today. Our Neighbor Mr Coig also. Papa has his seeder.

The pasture does not look as well as it should. It is badly cut up by the stock and last week, the cold wind blew a perfect gale and dried things out dreadfully. Yesterday and today have been very pleasant.

Uncle expects to start for the mines Monday. Papa isn't going now. Roscoe says the whole place is under snow and that they cant expect to do anything before April. He thinks uncle very foolish to go now.

You will probably be intrested in knowing that Grannis was appointed trustee last week. He feels that the responsibility of a large office now rests on his sholders.

All (or at least) quite a no. of Calabasas people were in L.A. last week on that Rankin and Branscomb affair and as it was postponed until the 14th they will have to go in again. I thought maybe you would be there as Foster inquired for your number. He served the papers here.

Now I have told you all the news except one thing, and that is that poor little Tip has his leg broken again, and it is surely bad this time. The bone sticks clear out. I try to keep splints on it but as I am not much of a Dr. do not do it well.

The little fellow is under my feet now. He is quite affectionate since he was hurt and seems to know when you try to help him.

Well my own dear Jack I have managed to write a long letter if there isn't much in it. And now I must close with my very best and dearest love. With lots of kisses now I'll still retain a good portion until I see you again.

Your own dear girl,

Katie

*written on ledger paper*

Pasadena

Feb. 3rd, 1895

My Dearest Katie:

I have just discovered that we are out of writing paper. But nevertheless—dear—I am going to write to you if I have to write on a board and send it by freight

I got a letter from Mr. Perret He says everything is all O.K. on the ranch. We have been looking for Frank home to stay If you get this scribbling before Frank comes home tell him that Mother would like very much to see him. And also tell him to come home in the express wagon as we need it.

Bert has been to the Island all week—expect him home tomorrow. I expect he is having a glorious time.

I am going to work for My Old girl Mrs. Flint next week. I have her Orchard to falow and some pruning to do for her. I expect to get a leg talked off of me. But I will be loaded for her. She is going to Los Angeles to live soon. So she says. Must be something in the wind.

Mother & I are keeping house alone now. We get along fine. She cooks. And you know what I do. We took a drive this afternoon. Went up to the Cemetery.[78] And all over town—and also made a call on one of our old time friends. This morning I passed reading the paper. And this eve I am spending with you as best I can—But it is an awfull poor way—.

I think I shall be out as soon as I finish Mrs. Flints orchard. Mr. Mundell is comeing out with me when I come out if he can. But I doubt if I make the trade and don't much care, for I think he wants something cheap. Honey I am much grieved to hear of poor Tip's misfortune. It is realy too bad. How did it happen—Hope you will be successful in healing it.

You also stated that Mr. Grannis was appointed to the honor of School Trustee. But did not say who had resigned. Allso was surprised to hear of your visitors— and that famous teacher of yours. He must be a peach if Tot is gone on him. What can he be made of, anyway.

---

[78] Probably to visit his sister Addie's grave.

I am glad he is a failure—for the sake of some of them cranks that allways wanted a man teacher.

Katie this is not much of a letter but don't know of a thing to write of interest to you. You write me a good long letter to make up for it, won't you, Jewell, and I hope this reaches you sooner than the last. If it don't I will get mad at Uncle Sam sure.

With all my love & Best Wishes.

I am your Jack

Good night

Darling P.S. Tell Frank to bring my mail with him when he comes if you see him. And be sure to bring the express wagon.

In mid-February Jack wrote that "my head is all awhirl." He had been offered two jobs: one, driving a butcher wagon; the other, driving rigs at the Raymond Hotel in Pasadena. There had been continued rainfall so that field work was impossible. Jack's brother Bert was already employed at the Raymond, and evidently had arranged for both Jack and Frank to be hired. Jack's conflict over taking the job stemmed from the fact that he would have no time off for two months and hence would be unable to see his Katie. She, however, assured him of her continuing love, and although Frank did not, Jack went to work at the Raymond.

The Raymond Hotel, completed in November, 1886, was the first of Southern California's large tourist hotels built during the boom of the '80s. Located in East Pasadena on the Raymond Hill, it overlooked the towns, fields, orange groves and vineyards of the San Gabriel Valley. Walter Raymond, the proprietor, and M. C. Wentworth, the manager, were able entrepreneurs who were clever enough to encourage the writing skills of George Wharton James in publicizing their resort. Although James was an important early portrayer of the Southern California landscape and wrote some worthy volumes (for example, *Through Ramona's Country*, 1908 and *In and Out of the Old Missions*, 1905), he was also once described as a "hotel tout," and he was the hired publicist for the Mt. Lowe Funicular and Hotel.[79] His description of the Raymond Hotel offers a rich sample of his style:

> It is not necessary that one should say the Raymond Hotel. The "Raymond" is enough. Everyone knows what you mean. There is but one Notre Dame, but one Acropolis, but one Colossus, and so there is but one "Raymond" when Southern California is mentioned.
>
> Many are not aware that had it not been for "The Raymond," many would never have seen the glories of Pasadena,—might never have heard of the protecting "mother mountains," might never have seen the Land of the Sun-Down Sea, for Messrs. Raymond and Whitcomb, when they decided to bring their thousands of cultured, refined and traveled tourists to Southern California determined to make a home for them whilst here.[80]

So much for an upstairs view of the Raymond Hotel. Jack Haas saw the hotel from the downstairs and gives us an earthier viewpoint:

---

[79]  Walker, pp. 147-149.

[80]  James, *Traveler's Handbook*, pp. 467-468.

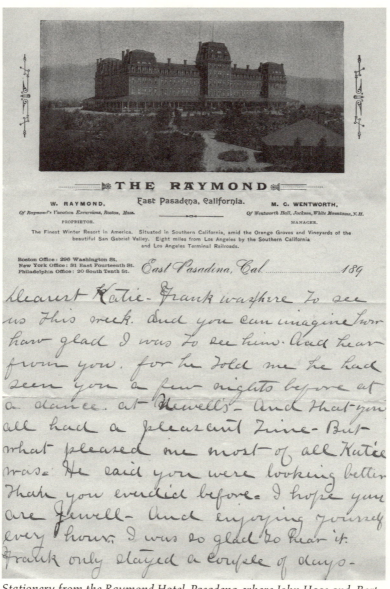

### THE RAYMOND
East Pasadena, California.

W. RAYMOND,
*Of Raymond's Vacation Excursions, Boston, Mass.*
PROPRIETOR.

M. C. WENTWORTH,
*Of Wentworth Hall, Jackson, White Mountains, N.H.*
MANAGER.

The Finest Winter Resort in America. Situated in Southern California, amid the Orange Groves and Vineyards of the beautiful San Gabriel Valley. Eight miles from Los Angeles by the Southern California and Los Angeles Terminal Railroads.

Boston Office: 296 Washington St.
New York Office: 31 East Fourteenth St.
Philadelphia Office: 20 South Tenth St.

*East Pasadina, Cal* .................... 189_

Dearest Katie- Frank was here to see
us this week. And you can imagine how
how glad I was to see him. And hear
from you. for he told me he had
seen you a few nights before at
a dance. at Newell's- And that you
all had a pleasant time- But-
what pleased me most of all Katie
was- He said you were looking better
than you ever did before- I hope you
are Jewell- And enjoying yourself
every hour. I was so glad to hear it.
Frank only stayed a couple of days-

*Stationery from the Raymond Hotel, Pasadena, where John Haas and Bert Perret drove fancy livery and rigs for wintering Eastern visitors*

Raymond Hotel

Pasadena

Feb. 22nd 1895

My Dear Katie—

As I did not get your letter for some days after it arrived
you will not get a reply as soon as I would like for you
to. But Dear we are kept so busy, and it is often very late
before we get in that it is impossible for me to go to the
Office when I would like to. I am driveing—You might
of known that for I am to lazy to do any work—as you
know. But you bet they keep us a jumping these fine days
as the house is chuck full and they all want to ride and
see the country.

Well Darling I am glad to know you are getting along
nicely. Jewel I can't half write tonight—as the electric
light is not extra just now—and we have no other. And
besides my arms are about pulled out from hanging on
the ribbons. I tell you Katie they have some fine turnouts
here. The finest I ever sat in—and plenty of them too.
We have about 73 head of horses to drive and they are
all out every fine day. It is quite a site to see the rigs go
out here in the morning just one continual string all the
time. It is a good place to work and we have a fine boss.
The best in the land. But I tell you unless a fellow can
drive them up in good shape he will never take out the
second rig—for them swells pay dear for their ride and
they want it in shape.

Mother is still nursing, so George Quigley told me. I
have not been home since I came here. And won't be able
to untill it rains again, which I hope will be soon for I
would like to rest one day—And write you a letter by

daylight and when I had time. I ought to have been in bed an hour ago, for we have to get up at five every morn and no Sunday—as that is our busiest day—So don't get discouraged if you don't get my letters regularly, dont think I neglect you. But write for it is such a comfort to receive your sweet letters. And some day I will repay you. So Darling with all my love and best wishes And Kisses.

I am your Jack

Katie, not to be outshone by Jack's sudden elevation to loftier surroundings, provided him with lively accounts of social life in Calabasas. There was the latest news about the school teacher, Mr. Swan, and although only a fragment of the letter remains, it goes right to the heart of the matter:

Leon broke the school up at 2 o'clock. The teacher had whipped a few kids and Leon took it to heart. He got a club and was going to do the teacher up, but they sent for Grannis and he had him (Swan) dismissed. So he bid Calabasas a joyous farewell this morn. I don't think there were any tears as he was surely a failure.

His successor is an elderly lady. Seems to be very capable. I hope she has no trouble as I think her a deserving woman.

A week later, Katie was able to report: "Everything at school seems quiet now. The teacher seems to have very little trouble."

She had other items of interest. There was to be a dance:

Ben Branscomb was here a few minutes ago and engaged the Schoolhouse for a Ball. To be Friday night. I wish you were here I would like to go for a little while and maybe I shall if you do not mind. But I'll find who the crowd is before I venture.

Her father had been absent: "Papa has just got home today from the law suit. He was delayed on acct. of sick headache." Her little dog, Tip, grieved her: "His leg is very bad and I fear he will either have to be killed or loose his leg. Poor little dog I hate to have him killed." Finally, there was a harbinger of spring: "I am going to gather some poppies after a while. The first of the Season." What pressed hardest on Katie's mind, however, is revealed at the beginning of her next letter:

Calabasas
Feb. 24 1895

My Dearest Jack:

'Tis just one year today, Jack, since we have been engaged. I wonder if you thought of it. I don't believe you did. What a long time to wait. When I think of it, it doesn't seem possible.

I do not feel like the person of last year. I felt then as though there was little pleasure in life but now I find so much. All I lack now to make me perfectly happy is you dear. And as I have your promise, I ought not to complain.

Well I wonder what you'll think when I tell you I danced until 1 o'clock Friday night. I surprised myself.

Frank came by and I went up with him. We had a first rate time. Everything was as quiet as could be as Branscomb & his followers were not there.

Your old friend, Nellie Bowen came out with Mrs. Grannis for the ball, but as Ben and Mrs. Grannis had a falling out the day of the dance neither she or Nellie came.

Harve Branscomb took her out riding early in the afternoon and they didn't get back until 10 o'clock at night and then he stayed at Grannises until 12. I guess they had a glorious time.

I hear that Bill Lee is to be married this week and is going to give a dance at Newells.

I miss you so much. Nothing seems the same without you. But never mind honey our day is to come and we will make it one long day of pleasure.

Frank had his picture taken out in the field where he was hearding horses. He was dressed just as he is when he is hearding and was on his pony. The boss and all the stock is on the same picture.[81]

They are trying to move the P.O. down to the Hall.[82] I expect they will succeed as they seem never to fail in any of their undertakings.

'Tis so hard darling to try and express on paper the feelings of my heart. There is so much I could say that I cannot write. But this much I can say that I love and

---

[81] That she would write in this way indicates how much a novelty and special occasion it was to have one's picture taken, especially when not dressed in one's best clothes.

[82] Apparently more machinations of the Branscomb gang.

wish and long for you every hour in the day and never forget you no matter where I am or what doing. Good by dearest.

> With my best
> and dearest
> love,
> Katie

While Jack held on to the ribbons and kept his long strenuous hours at the Raymond, Katie wrote faithfully, and at the end of February, she had an exciting story to tell: Harvey Branscomb had been stabbed three times by Manuel Dominguez. Her letter began with a little coquetry, but soon came to the big news:

I fear seeing so many pretty girls that you will forget your little country maid. I suppose you enjoy driving such nice horses, it must be quite a treat, even if it does make your hands tired. I wish I could see you drive once; you must look quite tony. I suppose Bert also enjoys the situation.

Well dearest it is time for me to be at my old job 'supper getting' so I'll say by-by for a little while and then give you some exciting Calabasas news.

After Supper, and back again. Aren't you glad to see me?

Well now for the news. You know there can be nothing very interesting without Branscomb is in it and it is he who has caused the excitement. I'll tell the story just as near right as I can. We have heard it so many different

113

ways that I really don't know just how it goes. It seems that Branscomb went to arrest Manuel Domingues for stealing a hog from Daly Nash and Manuel refused to go (so they said). So B. rushes on him and strikes Man—over the head with his revolver. The woman folks upon seeing this rushed between them, and Manuel took advantage of their temporary protection and reached around and stabbed Branscomb three times. Of course B—thought he was killed and told Bass, the fellow that's stopping with him, to shoot. So he shot at Manuel 3 times, two of the bullets took affect. The most serious one lodged in his leg or in the kneecap.

Branscomb had his usual crew along. They said when the fracas commenced there was a great—

Unfortunately, the rest of Katie's letter is lost, and her sentence will be forever uncompleted. We do know, however, that the excitement brought a deputy of law officers out from Los Angeles to Calabasas to investigate the affair, and on February 28, 1895, the *Los Angeles Evening Express* printed a full-column account. The headlines read:

### Dominguez Did the Stabbing
### Harvey Branscombe Gives His Version of the Affair and it is Corroborated by Most Witnesses
### Henry Bass of Artesia
### Was the Man who Shot Dominguez After He Stabbed Branscombe.
### Officers Return from Calabasas

Following this extended headline is a long account of the Los Angeles officers trying to get a death statement from Branscomb, who refused, claiming that he was not going to die. "He wanted his friends in Los Angeles to know that he would live to read many of their funeral notices yet."

Katie was wrong in only one detail. It was not one, but four, hogs which were in contention. According to the article, "The slaughtered carcasses of 4 porkers were seen by a brother of Constable Nash (George) at Dominguez' place, and it was this which had brought Branscombe and his men to the Dominguez." The report ends on an intriguing note: "During the excitement subsequent upon the encounter, the meat was spirited away and has not been found."[83]

The shoot-up must have infused new life into the settlement and no doubt was the chief topic of conversation at the dance which Katie attended the following Saturday.

> Calabasas
> March 5—95

My Dearest Jack:

I feel like writing this morning so will employ myself in writing to you. Yesterday and today seem very quiet after so much excitement. It seems rather plesant to have a breathing spell. Would you like to know how I have been employing myself the last few days? I am almost afraid to tell you for fear you'll think I am getting to be a regular gadabout.

I told you in my last letter there was to be a dance at Newells. Well Frank came up and we all went over. We had a great old time. We never got home until 4 o'clock next morning.

---

[83] *Los Angeles Evening Express*, February 28, 1895, p. 3.

There was preaching Sunday morning and in the evening also. So you see it kept me busy to get around in time to get there. It was a new preacher, a young man by the name of Watson.

Yesterday, owing to lost sleep and too much exercise, I felt, as Isaac expresses it, like a morning glory in the afternoon.

So you see my dear I have had no time to be lonesome (only for you) and I did wish so much for you. I miss you on every turn. It makes me feel like a stray. I feel quite guilty to be going so much and know that you are toiling.

I hear there has been a great deal said about the bravery of Mr. H.A. in the papers.

Thanks to the tender care he has received, they think he will live. What a pity! We could spare him so well. Some say Manuel will have to have his leg amputated, others say he will get out alright, which I think most probable.

Since they have both been laid up everything is quiet and peaceful.

It is too bad that spring, the prettiest time of the year, should pass away, and we not able to enjoy it together but I hope we both live to see and enjoy many together. And I think we shall if the Lord is willing.

Good by my own dear boy. With my very best love I am

Your ever loving

Katie

—Plenty of kisses—

A few days later, Katie wrote Jack another of her long letters, but all that remains is this:

. . .I also hear poor Tom Goss has passed away. Poor soul, he is at last free from the temptations he could not resist.

Branscomb is as well as ever. He wasn't as badly hurt as he thought. Henry says when he put him in the wagon to move him he told him to drive careful he only had an hour to live and he wanted to live in peace. I haven't heard from Manuel but guess he too is alright.

We received an invetation to a dance at Chatmans Friday night. I don't think I shall go as it is a long dark drive with anyone but you. If Frank should come up and want to go I'd go but hardly think he will. I'll have to see Frank and pump him about you as you did of me. I hope he didn't tell you how many times I danced with Bob Lee or you will be jealous. He seemed to be gone on me and I am sure I don't know why for I am surely not on him.

With my best and dearest love and plenty of kisses

I am Your Own,

Katie May. I. ?
(yes)


The furore over the Branscomb-Dominguez dustup gradually abated, and Katie resumed her recital of everyday happenings. Uncle Robert Shaw returned from his trip to the mines at Randsburg, and "...found things just as Roscoe told him. He says there is lots of money there but you can't do anything now." So with

117

the hope of golden riches once more gone a-glimmering, Uncle Robert and his son-in-law Ed Mitchell rented land in Lankershim and were going to put in a crop of potatoes and beans. Then there was brother Frank, who "got kind of used up he was riding a young horse and it nearly shook him to pieces. Mr. Perret said he was going home (i.e., Pasadena) if he did not feel better."

Jack meanwhile kept busy on his first month at a new job and wrote little. One page of a letter survives, however, which he must have written after a bad day at the Raymond:

Dear, I wish you could just see how people enjoy themselfs that have more money than they know what to do with. There is about 400 of them here—and they are the hob-nobs of the land I tell you. And them darned old women make me so tired—

They never know what they want. Always a kicking about something—the roads too dirty or too rough or afraid of the railroad for fear they would get thrown out and get their hair mussed and I don't know what—

Now, Jewell. Do write me often if you can for I cannot tell you how I long for your sweet letters. Oh, if I could only fold you in my arms tonight and get one of them sweetest of Kisses. It seems Dear that our lot so far has been a hard one. I could hardly realize it when you wrote me we had been engaged one year. But it is so. I hope that we can soon put a stop to this engagement by being made one. And we can, I know, and we will dear. For better or for worst.

Now, Angel, I must close and get ready to go out. And it is cold and foggy too, almost raining. I wish them old hags would drink so much tea that they won't be able to go out again for a month. So Darling good night with Love and best wishes from your

Jack

Address. East Pasadena

 Bye Bye Darling

Raymond Hotel


There had been wind and no rain in February. Katie had written that she looked forward to a rainy day for two reasons: one, because the wind was drying out the crops, and two, because she would get a nice long letter from Jack. Her wish was granted on St. Patrick's Day.

Hotel<br>
Raymond<br>
Pasadena<br>
3-17-95

Dearest Katie—

On this 17th day of Ireland, we were fortunate enough to have a shower of rain—and that gives me a chance to answer the many loving letters I received from you this last week.

I was down to L.A. Friday. And heard of your Father being there but could not find him. I would liked to have seen him very much—and had a chance to ask him how my Idol was getting along.

I wish I could drive up to the door and take you out for a drive with the team I had out today. It would be grand

119

Dear if we just had such an outfit to take in Calab with. We would make them Hayseeds open their eyes.

Was glad to hear that the stock are doing so well up there now. It will not be long Dear untill I will be able to be out there. Business is getting a little slack here allready and I am going to get off as soon as I can, for I am dieing by inches to see my Jewell. And get one—Yes—all you have of them sweet kisses you write about. I would have liked to have been there at some of those dances, for you know I love dancing better than any thing else. More especially if it's a long ways off—the place where the dance is, I mean.

Darling you write that you wish we were fixed so you would not have to treat this engagement as a secret. No one wishes it more than I darling. I assure you. And hope I will be able to have your wish granted mighty soon.

It has been a month day before yesterday since I came here. It seems like six to me. About 2 about 3 weeks more I will be through I think. . . have not seen Mother since I came. . .t is a shame but I cannot get away in the daytime. And don't like to be out all night. And she is not home anyway.[84]

Well darling I hear a racket over to the barn and expect I had better get over and help put away the stock—so my darling, I must close this scribbling—and get a move on me.

With all my best wishes and Kindest love

I am your<br>Jack—Sure

Bye-Bye Dear

---

[84] Mary Perret was still a nurse-midwife.

The rain brought an adventure for Katie with the new schoolmarm:

Calabasas
March 18—95

My dearest Jack:

I am a little late with my letter this week but couldn't very well help it.... I feel all used up today. The teacher went in on the cars Saturday and as the train does not run on Sundays I promised her I'd go to Aunts Saturday night and meet her next day at Hollywood at half past eleven. I kept my appointment but was not surprised that the old goose did not hers.

I went down to Overman's then, and waited until half past one.[85] She came on that car. It began to rain just as we left Hollywood and by the time we were over the Pass it was coming down in good style. Uncle would not hear of me coming on and as I was not anxious myself to brave the storm we camped there for the night and came home early this morning.

I caught cold in my eyes from the exposure, and I look like I'd been on a spree. The old lady can hunt up some other softy next time. She'll never catch this chicken again. She doesn't know enough to keep out of the rain when she can.

I hope my dear boy had one Sunday to himself. You surely had the afternoon anyway if it rained as hard there as it did at Lankershim. Aunt started yesterday

---

[85] The Overmans lived in Hollywood. Katie's aunt and Uncle lived in Lankershim.

for San Luis Obispo Co. to see Mary.[86] So everything was comparatively quiet. Flora had an interesting novel to read so she went and lay down in her room that she might not be disturbed, the teacher and Aunt played checkers. And I played with the babies. So passed the Sunday eve away.

How I wished darling to see you. It seemed you were so near and yet so far.[87] It seems that time passes so slowly. To me anyway. I guess though it doesn't hang on your hands you keep so busy.

There has been little of interest going on here of late. I did not go to the dance at Chatman's. The boys did. They said Frank was there.

I hear Mr. Richardson is going to bring his new wife home soon. I met him going to L.A. yesterday. Maybe he was going after her then. They say he will also have a stepdaughter of sixteen.

One of the Gibson boys axidentally shot Arthur Alf in the heel with a No. 22 rifle bullet. I guess nothing serious. And that is all the news I can think or know of that is worth writing

I am kind of a swindle dearest. I never can tell or show you how much I love you. Words and pen fail to express true feelings

From your own ever loving

Katie

---

[86] Mary Stratton, with whom Nettie had lived in Ventura. The chronology is confusing in this paragraph. Aunt had not yet left for her trip on the night Katie and the teacher were there.

[87] About twenty miles but by horse a good distance.

Katie's spirits were wonderfully lifted when she received the St. Patrick's Day letter from Jack, telling her that he would be in Calabasas in two or three weeks. She promptly replied:

Calabasas

March 24, 95

Dear Jack:

I could have shouted for joy when I received your last letter. To think you will not be away much longer was the best news I'd heard. I felt like sitting right down and answering it; but as I'd only written the day before I thought I had better wait a few days.

This is a beautiful day. It is far too nice to be indoors. I wish you were here. We'd try to work some scheme to take a drive.

Roscoe is here today. He has been here since Friday. He, Fred Grannis, Geo. Fooshee and Sam Hayes were all here Friday eve. We had quite a sing and as Isaac was feeling unusually gay he finished the entertainment.

Mr. Richardson is really married. You see we let him get ahead of us. But you see too they havent as much of their life before them as we have.

All the Calabasas lads shivareed him the night after their arrival. They say his frow is quite a talker.

. . . You said you wished you could take me out riding in a carriage such as you have there. I surely would enjoy the ride but I think I'd rather have the cash that they cost. I'd feel strangely out of place in such a rig. You forgot I guess that I am a hayseed too.

I did not mean dearest to annoy you by mentioning our engagement. I know you have enough worry besides that.

123

And I really did not mean to write it. It was a slip of the pen. So forgive me and I'll say no more.

I hear Bob Lee is going to give a dance in the school house Saturday night. I expect it will be a great affair. Dances seem to be all the go at present.

Well, Honey, I do not write to tell you the news but to assure you of my love. . .Write whenever you can to your own

Katie

Will is waiting to mail this and keeps hurrying me. Consequently it is poorly written.

Three days later, it rained again, and Katie and Jack each wrote a letter to one another on that day, Jack's containing the news of another offer of work.

East Pasadena,<br>Cal.<br>Mar. 27th, 1895

Dearest Katie:

We are haveing another of those spring showers. Which I am sure will be a great benifit—not only to us—But everybody I think I can enjoy it as much as anyone for the opportunity it affords one to write to you Dear.

I receive your letters regular now and am very glad indeed when I get them. The waiter girls bring them in the dineing hall and put them under our plates and Katie I cannot help it. But I look for one every time I eat.

I was up home and saw Mother a few nights ago. I had a party to the Hotel Green and had to wait for them until 11 P.M. so I went up and spent the eve. Mother is home

124

now. All by her lonesome. But is feeling well. I was not much surprised to hear of Richardson's marriage as I expected it some time ago. I suppose he will move up on the Fletcher place now. For that is what he was fixing it up for. I hope he will. That will give us some more new neighbors.

I have a good chance to go East with this outfit when this house closes. And drive for them in the White Mts. New Hampshire for the summer and then come back with them in the spring again. Won't that be fine. Have a good chance to take in the East and get payed for it. So I think I will get ready to go. They leave here about the first of May. But I guess not.

Darling if you could come along, I would be glad to go. But to leave you that far away—Never—No never. I can get along without seeing the East. But cannot without you. As soon as I can get off I am going west—as far as Calab. anyway.

But Jewell I hardly think I will be able to get away as soon as I expected for business is keeping up fine—And we don't have any time to spare in fine weather—And as long as that keeps up there is no chance to get off.

Katie you get after Isaac or Frank. And have them come to Los Angeles La Fiesta week for it will be grand. Well worth your while to see and then I can see you too— which will be nicer than the fiesta. If you could work it that way—and then let me know what night you would be there I could come down and see my Darling. Wouldn't that be fine....

It commences on the 13th and lasts one week. Come if you can. And then come over to Pasadena for a while. Well

125

Darling think it over and do the best you can…. Now Honey I must close. With a Kiss and fondest love

Jack

*In Isaac E.'s handwriting*

Calabasas,
California
Mar. 27/95

Jack dear,

I have been waiting ever since supper for the boys to get quiet so that I could collect my witts enough to write you a few lines. Every one is in bed now and I feel sleepy myself. So I'll not promise you a complete letter this eve but will finish tomorrow. The boys offered to write for me but as they neither knew who I was writing to or what about I thought I could do it best. You will see by the heading that Isaac started it for me. I shall look for another nice letter from my dear, soon, as this has been another wet day and I don't suppose you will have to be out all day.

I always feel so lonesome when it rains at night, that is, what time I'm not asleep. So you see I'm not lonesome long as I put in most of the night just that way.

It is coming down in good shape now. It has rained so hard this afternoon that the creek is running.

Papa & Isaac have been planting potatoes and corn for the last few days. They got them in just in time to get a benefit.

There was quite an excitement at Calabasas today. It

was the day set for Dominguese's trial but as he did not appear on the scene it was reset for Saturday. One of his lawyers was out and he said Manuel wouldn't be able to come out for 3 weeks.

Emmett Overman is stopping here now. He came bag & baggage yesterday. Guess from the looks of things he is going to stay until he finds something better.

And this dear is all the news I know of tonight except it be to assure you there is to be a dance in the school Saturday night. Unless I feel better by that time than I have for the last week I fear I'll not enjoy it much. I've had a dreadful cold, sore throat and sore eyes but they are all better now and I am on fair way to recovery.

Good night darling I wish I could kiss you & rest for just a minute on your dear brest.

Katie

April arrived, and Katie set herself the task of advising Jack on his immediate future and providing him with local news tidbits:

Calabasas
April 2 1895

My dearest Jack:

To say I was glad to hear from you again is a mild way of expressing it. I was delighted.

I am going to give you a little lecture and advise. Darling, you ought to accept and embrace the chance to go to the White Mts. Not for the gain but for your own gratification. You owe yourself that much. 'Tis the chance of your life-time. Remember, dear, that after you once become encumbered with a wife & other ties (perhaps in time), that then it cannot be. But now you are free and have the chance and you may never have either again.

I will be true as steel dearest and try to wait patiently until I feel that my turn has come.

Darling, I know how hard it would be to part for so long, but it seems equally as hard to think that I am the cause of you missing such a good chance.

Think very seriously over it Jack and do not let me be the cause of your staying, but remember we can love each other just the same.

I shall await a reply very anxiously. I wish I could see you and talk to you as I cannot tell you near as well on paper as I could by talking how much I'd like for you to go.

Honey, I have been trying to think of some way to take in the La Fiesta but to save me I can think of no way. Lillie[88] wanted me to spend that week with her which I could do, but I don't know how to manage to see my dear boy. I am very poorly prepared to attend but I'd go with the dress I have on if I thought I'd see you. Isaac has been scheming to go in also. He has secured the job of census Marshall but cannot commence before the 15th and I fear he will not get his money in time. Then you know he don't much like to be bothered with a sister. But I'll go if I possibly can. Maybe something will turn up before then. If so I'll let you know.

I have to go in before then if I can. I was going tomorrow

---

[88] Lillie Kettle of Colegrove, Katie's closest woman friend at that time, seems to have been the only person let in on the secret of Katie's engagement.

with Papa but he thought I'd better wait a few days. He has not got his money from Cheesebrough yet. He wants to be there tomorrow for that land case.

I got a letter from Lill yesterday. She said she expected to have called me Mrs. H before this. I feel like telling her I wish she could. She wrote and asked me if I didn't want to take her place, or the place where she has been working for a while as she is not ready to go back now and they don't like the girl they have. If I thought Mamma could spare me for a month I'd feel tempted to take it.

We still have the "Old Pelican," as the boys call the teacher, and suppose we will have until the end, which will be about the last of May. The Deputy County Superintendent of Schools stayed here last night and I think will be here for a day or so as he is visiting all the schools around here.

Tis the toughest school here you ever saw or heard of. They do just as they please—talk and laugh and fight, make fun of the teacher, holler at people, in and out of school alike. She has no more controle over them than the wind or Swan had.

We had a fine time at the dance Saturday night. The best yet. Frank came by as usual for me. Emmett honored me by asking for my company but I told him I had company engaged which was a little story, but I felt sure Frank would come if I waited long enough.

Sunday I took a long ride on Tene. Will & I called on Mrs. Richardson. I thought as they were to be such near neighbors that I'd get acquainted. You bet she's a talker. She can do enough for both. The whole kit of them are staying on the Fletcher place, 7 in all. I don't see how they manage as the house is not large.

Well, dear, if you have no time to write, you have no time to read either, so I'd better not write any more this time for fear you'll not read it all.

Now, are you real sure Johnny it is not the pretty waitress and not my letters you look so closely for. Well, I'll keep on writing just the same so as to be sure you'll not be dissapointed either way.

I'll try to meet you La Fiesta week if I can. Can you only get off at night? I want to see you so much. Good by dear, dearest Jack.

Write me an ans. as soon as possible as I want to know what you think of my proposition. With my best love and kisses and the hopes of seeing you soon. I am as ever your own

Katie

La Fiesta week was first held in 1894, organized by a group of Los Angeles businessmen to attract visitors to economically depressed Los Angeles. It proved so successful that in the years which followed it became a joyous spring celebration. Sarah Bixby-Smith [who wrote her memories of girlhood in Los Angeles in the '80's and '90's in a book called *Adobe Days*] recalled how the streets were lined with palms and the buildings adorned with red, yellow and green banners, the colors of La Fiesta. For a week bands played, people wore costumes ("Spanish cavaliers and senoritas appeared again in our midst"), and the fire horses were garlanded with flowers as they pulled the shining engines on parade. The great dragon emerged from Chinatown in procession with floats carrying "the bewitching little Chinese children wearing their vivid embroidered garments and beaded headdresses."[89] There was also a grand society costume ball at Hazard's Pavilion, at which a reigning Los Angeles society belle was chosen to be La Reina de la Fiesta. Although all this took place less than forty miles away from Katie in Calabasas, the life it represented was, in truth, as remote from her as the moon.

Calabasas

Apr. 6 1895

My dear Jack:

I shall endeavor, as best I can (with Isaac, Will, and Henry singing, drumming on the organ and cutting up as only they can) to start a letter to you—any way—I never feel satisfied unless I at least start a letter Saturday night as Sunday morning always slips away before I can get down to writing, consequently cannot do justice.

The boys have been trying all afternoon to fix your saddle and they are still at it. Isaac has it spread out on the floor trying to put the stirrups on, for that seems to be the trouble.

His temper was just about to get the best of him, but he has just announced that he has succeeded in getting it right.

Such a dreadful old day this has been dear! The wind has been blowing dreadfully all day but has gone down now. Every one seems cross, but I suppose it is my own cranky

---

[89] Sarah Bixby-Smith, *Adobe Days*, Cedar Rapids, Iowa, The Torch Press, 1926, pp. 161-62.

self that makes others seem so. I have felt so miserable the last few days that I excuse myself on those grounds. I had quite a seige with my throat and eyes.

I thought my throat was much better, but today it is hard for me to talk or eat. I have been doping it with all kinds of truck so it ought to be well tomorrow.

I can't go riding tomorrow as Isaac says I shan't put my old saddle on any of the horses again, as it makes their backs sore, and I guess it does. I'll have to wait until you come home and we'll find some way to ride won't we darling.

My dearest Jack I do fear I'll not get to the Fiesta. Papa has been in town since Tuesday and I expected to have gone in before this. Isaac is talking of giving up the Fiesta and going with Henry and Sam on a camping expedition to the Tujuna Canyon. So we are undesided as yet what to do. I don't mind missing the Fiesta, for I'm used to missing such things, but 'tis you my own darling, that I miss seeing. I used to think it a long time when you went to town for a few days but not to see you for three months seems much longer.

Well, dearest Jack, I know it is long past bedtime for me so I must bid you good night. With my fondest love and kisses and everything else I am ever your own

—Katie—

Sunday Morn

Well, dearest, today is a decided change from yesterday. 'Tis a lovely day. One could not feel cross today if they tried with the birds singing, the flowers blooming and everything to make one happy.

The boys are out capturing their steeds. I suppose they are out for a show today. And you will be to, won't you dear? I envy you today as it is much too nice to stay indoors.

I think Papa has deserted us. He is not home yet. I must not forget to tell you that the P.O. has been moved again. The Hon. H.A. now presides I believe. They have it in the courthouse I hear. I suppose our letters will be safe there, don't you think? If not we'll have them come to Daices.[90]

I was very glad to hear that Mrs. Perret is well. I was afraid she'd overwork and have to go home sick.

Mama's arm is getting better, now that warm weather is coming on.

Aunt hasn't got back yet or hadn't the last time I heard. She said in her last letter that Mary was some better and they were going to send her to some hospital, but it is hard to tell anything about the case from what she says.

Max Bly is "forman" of a ranch of his fathers now out near Burbank. His father sold out his shop and bought a farm. Good for Max!

Roscoe and Emmet Overman are over at F. Grannises cutting wood—Quite a fall for a man with a mine isn't it. Roscoe has another little girl of a few months.

How much I wish to see you today dear. I'm afraid I'll not know you if I don't see you soon. Frank told me you looked quite gay with your outfit. I'm afraid you'll not want to ride in a cart again. No—I'm not

[90] The Calabasas P.O. must have moved as often as a floating crap game during this period. The Daices had a sub-station near Las Virgenes Canyon.

dear—afraid of any of these things I just said it to be saying something.

I hope I get a letter soon as I cannot help looking for them even if it does not rain—Well dearie I must say by-by for this time. Hoping to hear from you or see you very soon. I am your own Hayseed. As you used to like to call me.

Katie may have abandoned her hopes of attending La Fiesta, but she did not give up in her attempt to see Jack. As the two following, and final, letters reveal, she was to be disappointed yet again.

Calabasas
April 11-95

Dearest Jack:

I am a little early with my letter this week but I wanted to drop you a line to let you know that I expect to be in L.A. next week. I intend going to Lillie's for a few days and then I may go over to Pas—I don't know how to make arrangements to meet you as I cannot tell how I shall go in, how long I stay or anything about it. I have a weeks furlough, as it is Institute week also and the teacher will not be here, and I am going to spend it away from here some way.

I have been waiting all week for a line from you hoping it would enlighten me as how to proceed.

I'll probably be at Kettles 2 or three days, and if you drop me a line there, as soon as you get this, and tell me when you can be off duty for a little while and where and how to meet you I'd be glad or if you think best to

134

wait until I go to Pasa and see me there or anyway you want dearest just so as I can see you. I'd go to no end of trouble to meet you, for as I have set my heart on seeing you & I'd feel most awfully dissapointed, and that I had my trip for nothing if I did not.

Isaac went hunting with the boys, as I told you he was going to, and what do you think! He killed 2 deer yesterday morning, within a hundred yards of each other. Geo. Nash had to go up there to get Henry as a witness on that Dominguez case, for it comes up again today, and he brought one home. 'Twas quite a treat. I wish you were here to share it. They say they will not be satisfied with anything less than a bear now. But I have doubts as to that.

Dear dearest Jack as I hope to see you soon I'll not tire you with a long letter, but just send my love, best wishes, kisses, etc. I am ever yours

Katie

P.S. If you write to Colegrove put in care of Miss Lillie Kettle as Ill be more apt to get it.

April 13 1895

Dear Katie—

No doubt you have been expecting this letter long ago and I feel guilty for not writeing. It seems a very funny excuse when I tell you I am so busy I cannot write—for I am sure I ought to be glad to be able to have such a darling to write to.

But Dear it will be only a short while now till we can talk with each other. And that will beat writeing all to pieces.

The house closes on the 22nd and then I will be done sure—if not before. I expected to be fired before this but the boss asked me if I would stay. As he had others he wanted to fire. And of course I had to say yes. Bert is not here any more. He was let out this week and two other fellows. So we are not so many now, and I expect next week will make a big change in business.

Darling you write that I had better go east while I have a chance. But I don't see the chance as you do. Just think, go now and come back next Dec. Oh—No. I have not got backbone enough to stand that long a separation, if it was only for 2 or 3 months I would go. The boss was at me again night before last to go with him. He would give me a job with him. That is as good as $50.00 a mth. and found,[91] and see me back next winter. But I told him No, I could not as I had something in this state that beat a job all to pieces. Then he said well Jack as soon as I land in Cal. next winter come and go to work for me. He told me I could have a chance any time I call on him. So Katie I feel good over it to think I gave him good satisfaction. For it is pleasanter to leave a place and know you are welcome back than to leave because the boss says so.

Well Honey I may be out there next week but don't look for me. I think the livery business will be done in a few days, but it may hold out to the last. Sorry to hear that you can't be in town for the Fiesta. But it may be for the best. Who knows?

Well darling I am glad that you get a chance to take in a dance and a horseback ride once in a while—for I am sure it would be lonesome for you to stay at home all the time.

[91] Room and board.

I will be glad myself when I get off here as it is awfull steady. And I have staid at my post at all times—Day and night. Tonight I am off. But tomorrow night I am good untill 11 P.M. alright if not later. But I am use to it and it don't bother me any more. I rather like it.—

The rest of the letter is lost, but we know that Jack never went back to the Raymond, because on the following afternoon, Easter Sunday, April 14, 1895, the Hotel Raymond burnt to the ground. No lives were lost and no injuries sustained, but the shock and loss to Pasadena were devastating and Jack's prospects with the hotel were gone. If he did help in the cleanup after the fire, it is unrecorded. What is certain is that on November 16, 1895, John "Jack" Haas and Katie May Ijams were married in Pasadena and came to the ranch in Calabasas to begin their married life. The long engagement was over.

*Wedding portrait of Katie Ijams and John Haas, married in Pasadena on November 16, 1895. She was 19 and he 28 years of age*

## ADDIE & EDITH
## (1896-1912)

### BIRTH OF ADDIE

NO ONE COULD SAY, as Nettie had of the Browns in Newhall, that Jack and Katie were "the 'softest' couple it was ever my lot to see." They had weathered childhoods of hardship and emerged as stable young adults willing to accept the responsibilities of creating a strong family and contributing service to their community. One year after their marriage, Jack drove Katie once again to his mother's home in Pasadena to await the birth of their first child. Twelve days after their arrival, on November 22, 1896, with her mother-in-law Mary Perret attending as midwife, Katie was delivered of a healthy baby girl. She was to be named Addie Camelia in honor of the deceased sisters of her parents (Camelia was the middle name of both Nettie and Edith Ijams).[92]

A few days after the birth, Jack returned to the ranch in Calabasas, and while Katie remained with the new baby in Pasadena, he wrote to her the news of home. Although the affairs of Jack and Katie had changed greatly in a year's time, life in Calabasas wagged along in its customary rhythms:

---

[92] Addie's birth was not recorded. Neither she nor her siblings had birth certificates.

Edith with her endless chicken dinners, Uncle Robert with his dreams of gold, the flareups of quarrelsome neighbors, and always the hard work and the wind. What also remained constant was Jack's loving devotion to Katie. If they had held the traditional hope that the firstborn be a male, he carefully reassured her that the birth of a girl was truly a blessing, and the reasons he gave imply much about the role a female was expected to play in a frontier settlement.

*Katie as a young mother*

*Addie Camelia Haas, first child of Jack and Katie, born in Pasadena November 26, 1896*

The following letter was written on a Sunday, one week after the birth of Addie:

Calabasas
Nov. 29th
1896

My Dearest Wife—

This has been one of the most disagreeable days I have experienced for some time. The wind has been blowing a hurricane all the day—and it has been cold. Your Pa & Uncle Robert were down to see me this morn. And I went home with them and had a chicken dinner with your Mama.

Uncle Robert looks much better than he did when he left and says he feels better than he has for years. I was quite surprised to see him looking so well. He did not make anything on the trip but his improvement in health was well worth the time it cost him. He says that great town of Randsburg is not up to much at present but will be a good camp some day—as there is Rich rock there but no way of milling it at present.[93] Hence there is no money made now. And a poor man can't stay there long as everything is quite high. Water is worth 4 ¢ a gallon and hay $30.00 pr Ton. And everything in proportion. He is trying to rent the Foreman Orchard this year. And if he gets that he wants Isaac to go in with him—and take half—as there is 80 acres and that is more than he can handle alone. He wanted to get a horse from me today for Ed Mitchell —he is moving from the place he is on and rented a small alfalfa ranch and needs another horse—but I have no old horse I could let him have at present but would give him a colt if he could do no better. But Uncle Robert thinks he can get him all the horses he wants from Frank Clapp. I was sorry for I would like to help Ed if I could. I told him that in the spring I thought I could spare him one after I had the crop in—if he still needed it. Old Buck is going to live and come around all right again She is as well as ever—but pretty thin. I thought sure she would be dead

---

[93] Eventually stamp mills were built for the area, and later tungsten and silver were discovered there. Neither Uncle Robert nor Isaac enjoyed the profits of these findings, however.

when I got home, but she fooled me.

If this horrid wind would stop blowing—And it would get warm we would soon have some feed.

## Second Edition

I was sorry to hear of so much sickness at home and hope the folks are well again now. And Darling do take care of yourself until I get home. Then I will take care of you. I hope my Dear Baby girl has been better since Sunday. And that she does not bother her Mama as much as she did. She must grow good as well as pretty. Isaac got a letter from Will yesterday. And he congratulated us for the baby being a girl instead of a boy. He is getting along fine, is at Capistrano Hot Springs—and wrote that he had just had a bath—and it made him feel like a new man. Frank was up to see me Sunday. He too is tickled over the baby being a girl. He said that is just what we needed, a girl in the family. So I guess we pleased all the boys—And more than pleased ourselves. I think baby will be made quite a pet of by her Uncles and I am not sure but what Papa will spoil her a-petting her.

I wish I could be with you now Honey. No doubt I could help you some. Besides being company. I am glad your Breast is getting better for it must have been very painfull.[94] But Darling bear it as best you can, and some day you will be rewarded for it. When Baby grows up she will make up for it. I have since the Baby has been born felt glad she came a girl, for you are the one that really needs her—you can raise her and take care of her better than you could a boy.

---

[94] Katie had problems with lactation. This disorder was some kind of a congestion or infection of the mammary glands. She used to put it bluntly, "My breast was caked."

Tell Mother when I come in I will plow that land and if I can get some one to take care of the place I will plow the orchard also. As it needs a plowing now. Frank is talking of quiting the ranch and comeing to town and going in business. He did not say when but not untill after plowing time anyway.[95]

Well Darling with my love and Kisses to you and Baby.

I remain yours

John Haas

Eleven days later, Jack wrote again to explain why he could not get away from Calabasas. Jack's in-laws at times must have taxed his sweet nature to the cracking point. He is known to have suffered from migraine headaches, and the situation in which he found himself in the early weeks of December must have been frustrating enough to bring on an attack. Perhaps writing all about it to Katie helped to ward one off.

Calabasas

Dec 10th 1896

My Dearest Wife—

Darling you write that you are very lonesome and homesick. I know it is a tedious wait for you. Besides feeling so poor. And not getting your rest of nights. It is sure a hard luck. But keep up your courage Dear. And I hope you will soon be able to enjoy life again. You ask me to come in Sat. But Darling I cannot as your Folks

---

[95] This came to nothing. Frank Perret lived the rest of his life in Calabasas.

are all going to your Uncle's Sunday. Their land case comes up Tuesday and your Father and Mother are going as far as Robert's. Then your Dad is going to town Monday morn.[96] Your Father said he would come and see you Monday night. And your Mother is comeing to Los Angeles Tuesday morn with Robert. Isaac & Will Johnson are going in together and I suppose I will have to take care of the stock while they are gone.

And Honey I am very busy putting in the crop. If the weather holds off dry next week, I will finish. The land is in the best of shape to work. And I would like to finish if possible. But if it should come a rain I will be in with you sooner. And if I can finish putting in the crop and can get some one to stay and tend to the stock, I will stay with you untill you are able to come out. You wrote that you were in town just a mth Sunday. It seems the longest month I ever put in. I had not kept track of the time but thought sure it was longer than that.

Your folks are quite busy getting ready for their trip and I hope it will be a successful one.

This is a conundrum.[97] It reads like one anyway. But you will understand what I am trying to tell you—I know.

If they did not have to go to town, I would have come in Saturday night—and come out again Monday. But Darling it seems allmost impossible for me to get away

---

[96] I could not find out about this; the case had something to do with a party named Cretzner, but whether it was about property in Calabasas or Toluca, I do not know.

[97] A puzzling question or a problem. Quandary more accurately describes Jack's attempt to explain the contingencies of his life at that moment.

now. The stock are running all over the County trying to get something to eat. The grass is started but so short that they cannot get it. The dry north wind has been blowing again ever since Sunday. It calmed down some today and I hope it is over with for it just drys the ground out and kills the young grass. Well Darling I have written you all I know. And can think of. Except that Mrs. N. Cooken has a baby; and that Richardson has taken all the work away from Branscom and given it to Daly Nash. I suppose there will be another war here soon. But Rich is loaded for him.

Honey I will expect an answer from you as soon as you are able to write. Tell me all about yourself—And our dear baby. Have her write to her Papa also—and don't forget to kiss her for me whenever you get a chance. Let me know how Mother and Bert are getting along. Give my love to all—

And with best wishes and love to you and Baby—

I remain Your dear Husband

John Haas

Good Night Darling—

And the wind still blows.

*Second Edition*

I got home Friday night just at dark. And I was most froze to death. It was awfull cold all day. I got along fine with the colts—when I got on this side of Burbank I turned the little mule loose and he followed fine—and the others led well. They did not seem to get a bit tired.

145

Bessie Settle is come out to see her dear Bro. Mike Wednesday. And I have to get her at the depot. I wish she would come when I was not quite so busy. I am going to plowing in the morning. I would like to sow and plow it under. But if this wind continues will have to plow and sow after a while.

Prof. Greve had Mike Stausen arrested for calling him foul names—and useing very bad language in his presence. The cause of the Trouble was the line fence between them. I have a lot of attachment papers to serve on Thorpe from Wilkerson of Colegrove but I don't know what to do untill I hear from Wilkerson again. For he left the papers here while I was in Town and expected to see me there. And did not so I don't hardly know what to do.

Your Mother is getting along well. And was quite pleased to see Uncle R. Bert has got a sore hand and has been on the retired list, but is some better. He had a boil, I think it was, on the back of his hand and it was awful sore. And has not been able to do anything—but is going to plowing as soon as able. Your Pa is going to Chatsworth tomorrow to try and get his seed grain. (And still the wind is whistling)

Well Darling I hope you have not got this wind in town And hope tomorrow the day you had set to get up will be a fine one. And do hope you have been getting along nicely—and that Sweet Baby girl of mine is going well and not keeping Mama awake too much at nights. Everybody is anxiously awaiting the arrival of you and our dear daughter here—And no one half as much as myself. They are getting up a Xmas tree here in the School house—And would like very much to have you here to help arrange matters. I told them I wish you were but that you could take no part in the tree if you were—

On Friday, a week before Christmas, Jack wrote in a near-desperate state of mind from the Ijams ranch. His exasperation with the Ijams can scarcely be contained, and the arrival of the gypsies must have been the final aggravation. The unintentional humor in the last paragraph can only be the product of someone who does not have his mind fully upon what he is writing.

Calabasas

Dec 18th 1896

My dearest Wife

I expected to be with you before this. But it seems that I am nailed to Calab. The folks all went away Monday and left me in charge. Isaac expected to get back Tuesday evening. And then I intended to go and see you.

Here it is Friday and no one in sight. But will come as soon as some of the folks get home. I am in a great fix this morning. Last night when I got here there was a band of Gypsies camped out here in front of the house. And of all the racket you ever heard they made it. I think they were all drunk. And I had to stand guard nearly all night for I knew they would steal everything on the place if they were not watched. And as soon as daylight this morn, they came prowling around. First the women came and wanted hay and barley and every thing they saw. But I refused them everything. And pretty soon the men came and wanted to buy hay for there horses. But I told them I had none to sell. And they are prowling around yet trying to get some. And here it is ten o'clock and no sign of them moveing yet. And I dare not leave untill they do. And I am so anxious to get home and go to work. I think I shall go out as soon as I get this letter written and order them off.

I hope some of the folks came to see you while they are in, for I am sure they have time enough. They have been gone long enough to make a ranch for them and Cretzner too. They will surely be home today. And if so I can come down imeadeatly. I have all arrangements made to leave.

Well Darling I hope you and baby are getting along fine. And will be well and everyone else when I get home. Nothing of importance happened around here since I last wrote you except Dr. Allen was convicted as charged by Mrs. Bentley and gets his sentence today and he will get a couple of years in state prison no doubt. And Charly Bell lost his arm. He got it shot off in a winery at Cucamonga.

With love and Best wishes dear.

And Kisses to you and Baby from your

Beloved
Husband Jack

Presumably the gypsies left and the Ijams returned with Jack's buggy in time for him to fetch Katie and baby Addie home for Christmas.

## GROWING FAMILY

With the birth of Addie the letters stopped and the

*Edith May Haas, born February 20, 1898*

*Earl Marion Haas, born March 23, 1900*

*The home place of the John Haas family, about 1905. Left to right: Valentin Haas, Katie Haas, John Haas, Charley Cheney and Bert Mesa (workers); in front, Edith, Earl, Addie Haas and their dog Shep*

*John and Katie Haas with Addie, Edith and Earl, about 1903*

busy years of building a life together began for Jack and Katie. Fifteen months after Addie's birth arrived the second daughter, Edith May, on February 20, 1898. Finally, two years later was born a son, Earl Marion, on March 23, 1900. The family was now complete, and Katie often remarked that she had had all her babies before her twenty-fourth birthday.

During the four years of Katie's childbearing, changes occurred in both the families and settlement of Calabasas. Foremost was the beginning of the three-year drought mentioned earlier in the book. In the years from 1896 to 1899, the annual rainfall was less than eight inches, and in the worst year, 1898, there was only five and a half inches of rain. James Guinn, the pioneer historian of Southern California counties, maintains that these dry years, although registering less rainfall than the droughts of the '60's and '70's, "produced little loss of stock for want of feed and very little suffering of any kind due to these dry years."[98] Maybe. But he certainly overlooked Calabasas when he wrote that statement. We have Isaac E.'s earlier description of the Valley during those three years when hopes dried up as did the land. He also described the old road from Cahuenga Pass to Encino (now Ventura Boulevard) as a "dustchoked trail used almost entirely by those who were heading out of the Valley driving their stock."[99] Pierre Agoure, one of the large landholders and stockmen west of the Calabasas area, lost 8000 head of sheep in 1898.[100]

Joe Russell of the great cattle ranch on the Conejo, the

---

[98] Guinn, Vol. I, p. 388.
[99] *Valley Times*, 1 October, 1945
[100] Guinn, Vol. II, p. 1636

Russell Ranch, recalled in his book of reminiscences that his father in 1897-98 decided to sell his cattle and not even try to carry them through the season. He also recalled that a ranch owner his father knew claimed that he'd never had to move stock from his ranch because of drought. Later, when Mr. Russell questioned another rancher about the truth of his claim, he was told that the rancher had told the truth: he had never moved his cattle. "He just let them die."[101]

Drought and discontent drove the Ijams from Calabasas, and in 1899, they at last moved to their land in Toluca (now Studio City) where they enjoyed better days. With the hard work of Isaac E. and Willie, they developed their 105 acres. Leasing an additional 1200 acres in the hills from J. B. Lankershim, they ran their cattle there and also took in horses and stock for grazing on a rental basis. In 1907 when an account of Isaac's life appeared in Guinn's *History of California*, the article stated that his 105 acres contained a house, barns and a windmill; sixty of the acres were planted in fruit orchards (walnuts, peaches, pears, apples and prunes). He also had twenty head of work horses and fifteen head of cattle.[102] Isaac moreover had been appointed the first justice of the peace in Toluca, and it was at this time that he acquired the honorific of "Judge," by which he was known for the rest of his life.

Katie had now cast her lot in Calabasas with the Haases and the Perrets. There were to be no rambling days for her such as her mother had known; her babies would never be put in a wagon and moved on to the next settlement. When

---

[101] J. H. Russell, *Cattle on the Conejo,* Los Angeles, CA, The Ward Ritchie Press, 1957. p. 66.
[102] Guinn, Vol. II, p. 1619.

Addie and Edith were sent to Pasadena, it was not to work in fruit harvests as their mother had, but to attend high school. Katie was ambitious for her children as well as herself. Proud and strong-willed, she fought all her life anything which degraded or demeaned her: the serving maid's attic, the shabby life in Ventura. She was a hard worker and given her limited sphere, she did exceedingly well. She knew her worth. For those who fancy such notions, she was born in the sign of Taurus, of the earth and tenacious.

After toughing it out in the last years of the nineteenth century, Jack was able to celebrate the arrival of the twentieth with a new job which assured him an income not dependent upon dry farming: he was appointed a Road Overseer by the Los Angeles County Board of Supervisors. Until his death he held this appointment, and one of the accomplishments during his tenure of office was to build the Old Topanga Canyon Road, which connected Calabasas with the Topanga Canyon Road leading down to the coastline. His keeping of books and conduct of business was scrupulous, and his skill in handling stock and dealing equably with men earned him his long tenure. Katie can also receive some credit, too, as the job was a political appointment and in order to see that a candidate favorable to their cause would be elected, election rallies were held in the schoolhouse to woo voters with speeches, songs, and food. Katie provided food—and abundantly. Addie remembers her mother baking ten or more cakes in the old wood stove a day or two before a rally. Evidently the combination of Jack's qualifications and Katie's cakes turned the trick. He held the job for seventeen years and at the time of his death had just been promoted with an increase in salary. Jack also dry-farmed grain crops on his ranch, boarded stock from a livery stable in Pasadena, and maintained and broke his own horses.

Jack's father Valentin lived with them, and although he had his own quarters in a little cabin set behind their house, he took his meals with them and was a full member of the household. Addie remembers the old man helping out with the family wash in the yard by turning the crank which churned the clothes in a primitive washing machine. In the early years he also drove the mail in a little cart and horse from Calabasas to New Jerusalem. At times he must have been a sore trial to his daughter-in-law. Once when she was gone for the day, he undertook to help by taking all the knives from her best silver plate flatware and sharpening them on a grindstone. When Katie returned and found her ruined knives with their blackened edges, she was wild with rage and grief. The old man, genuinely confused, had thought he was doing her a good turn because, as he told her, they were not sharp enough.

His grandson Earl used to remember with amusement that if someone came to the ranch when only Grandpa Haas was there, wanting to look at a horse that might be for sale, he would lead the prospective buyer out to the corral or barn, regaling him along the way with all the beast's shortcomings. Or if it was hay for sale, then he would point out its poor qualities. In retrospect there is a poignancy about the life of this old man, and Addie remembers with remorse how unmercifully they had teased him as children. Earl once told of stealing and hiding his wooden leg which he had removed during a siesta in his cabin. When sufficiently outraged, he would swear at them in German.

In addition to Grandpa Haas there were other relatives living nearby. Jack's half-brother Frank Perret lived a couple of miles down the road from the Haases, across the way and a little east of the schoolhouse. His first wife Pearl was a local girl and their daughter Minnie was born about the same time as Earl. Pearl died young and Frank's second wife Viola (always known as Ollie) helped raise the little girl along with Grandma Perret in Pasadena. Frank had no children by his second marriage, and he lived and died in Calabasas.

At the turn of the century Mary Perret acquired the Calabasas store and post office. The original store had been built by one Mike Lordon in 1890 near the Ijams homestead, and he had been friendly with Isaac and his family. About two years after founding the store, he was shot dead by a customer in an argument over a bill. His brother and sister came from the East to take over the enterprise, but then sold out to Mary Perret, who later added more rooms across the back to accommodate more guests. Interestingly enough, her second husband John Perret came out to Calabasas to run the store and spent the rest of his life there, ending his days with son Frank. Edith remembers that during her childhood Grandpa Perret lived alone in a little cabin back in a canyon, and he too drove the mail from Calabasas to New Jerusalem. Once, driving a little horse named Mupsie, he was in a terrible accident on the Conejo and Mupsie was killed.

Mary Perret, having consigned her second husband to Calabasas, remained in Pasadena with her son, Bert. He had married Dolly, the school teacher at Catalina Island of whom Jack wrote in one of his letters to Katie. She was older than Bert; indeed had once been his teacher in school in Pasadena before she went to Avalon. After her early death from tuberculosis Bert married a Swedish lady named Gertrude, who is chiefly remembered for having always kept a pot of hot coffee on the stove to serve visitors. They had three children and were Christian Scientists, Bert eventually, becoming a reader in the First Church of Christian Science in Pasadena. Handsome Bert seems to have been his mother's favorite, so perhaps it was he who persuaded Mary Perret to embrace the teachings of Mary Baker Eddy.

It is a curious fact that, although Mary Perret seemed to give unstintingly of her time and energy to others (boarding the Ijams children, nursing and midwifing, babysitting grandchildren), the family memories of her are neither sunny nor tender. No little tales from her granddaughters of ice cream treats, picnics, nor even laughter or silly chatter as they worked in her kitchen or rode along with her in the horse and buggy; she comes down to us as a relentless figure, bundled in black, pursuing Paul's instruction to the Corinthians to "Run, that ye may obtain," and neglecting his later warning that all gifts, however excellent, are worth nothing without charity, "which suffereth long and is kind."[103]

Her conversion to Christian Science did not mellow her, as Addie's following grim remembrance will attest:

> I don't know when Grandma Perret became a Christian
> Scientist, but she was one when I went to high school. And
> I had boils when I was in there. The diet she had—she'd
> give us pancakes for breakfast and if we didn't eat them

---

[103] I Corinthians, ix, 24 and xiii, 1 & 4.

all, she'd cut them in strips and fry 'em at noon and we'd have them for lunch. And I got these awful boils and she wouldn't [provide medical aid]—I remember she used to tell me to take a bottle and put over them for suction—I don't know—put hot water in the bottle to try to draw out these boils.

I went to the Christian Science Sunday School and Church in the two years I lived in Pasadena—and they didn't make a Christian Scientist out of me.[104]

This was the array of relatives surrounding Addie, Edith and Earl Haas during their childhood years as they grew and thrived. Although they had some of the usual childhood diseases such as mumps and whooping cough, they were spared the more dreadful ones such as diphtheria and typhoid which children in the more populous and less sanitary downtown area of Los Angeles were subject to. In either 1903 or '04, however, a crisis of sickness struck all three families (Ijams, Haas and Perret), one of those periods in which life seems to move under a dark cloud and remain there. The only record of it is found in six notes written by Katie, pencil-scribbled on scratch paper from Toluca. They were never sent, but Katie preserved them, indicating that they had a special significance for her.

She had been called down to Toluca to nurse her brother Willie, then in his mid-twenties and who, according to the memory of his youngest son, Robert Ijams, was dangerously ill with "double pneumonia." Edith Ijams, old, not in the best of health herself and apparently never too good around the

---

[104] Tape interview with Addie Haas Mulholland, 6-22-76.

sick, was delegated to go to Calabasas to take care of Addie, Edith and Earl while Katie nursed Willie.

In addition to Willie's bad case, Frank's wife Pearl was ailing in Calabasas, and Dolly, Bert's wife, had come out from Pasadena to attend her and look after little Minnie. It is possible that the illness which afflicted Pearl at this time resulted in her death. In any event she did not live long after this time. Dolly also was to die shortly after. The Haas family was not exempt either: the children evidently had swollen neck glands, and even durable Jack had a bad cold. Only Katie seemed to soar above the plagues and fevers of the time. She wrote in one of her notes that she felt fine, adding the telling comment, "It just seems strength is given me." For all her life, this would be a true saying.

Several letters reveal this time:

Note 1

Toluca

Saturday

8 A.M.

Dear Jack,

The Dr. is here this morning and is going to hand this note to the train man. As far as we would be able to judge there is not much change in Willie but the Dr. says his indications are all favorable, his lungs are now in a condition to heal. I was up until 4 this morning. He rebelled at having me at first but we have established a good understanding now.[105]

---

[105] Anyone who ever had a taste of Katie's admonishing tongue can imagine how that understanding was arrived at. I recall when I was nine years old and staying with her for a visit. As we did the dishes together I told her a little joke that was going the rounds on the playgrounds of my school and which I thought hilarious, although its mildly salacious overtones had eluded me.

Let me hear from you. The Dr. is going to fix some med. for Earls neck and Ill send it soon.

I must hurry this so no more at this time.

Love and Kisses to all,

Katie

Note 2

Sunday

Dear Jack,

I am afraid I have not succeeded in getting word to you very well but it seems I have no oppertunity to send word. The Dr. tells me he did not get my note in time to go up yesterday.

Willie's condition is very favorable at present. He is sweating something dreadful but that is one of the symptoms. We have to keep him rubbed down all the time. The fever is receding and he is liable to be much weaker after but the Dr. says everything is happening just as it should. He seems very much pleased that I am here. He says to Will this morning there has been a big change in the appearance of the family since your sister came. I hope things at home are fareing as well.

It is pretty hard to have the strings pulling so hard both ways. My mind is at home and my hands here. I will get released just as soon as the Dr. will consent. Unless of course the children are sick. And then I'll come. Give

---

Unwittingly I had overstepped the bounds of decency with her. Her hands stopped their action in the soapy dish water and turning her eyes upon me, she quietly said, "Why, Catherine, I am surprised at you." That was all, but if she had pounded me through the floor I was standing on, she could not have hit me harder as the full implication of my little joke suddenly flooded in on me. Her words bore weight. She had, in a word, authority.

my love to Pearl & Dolly and tell them I hope they are both still improving.

Love and best wishes to babies Papa & all—

Katie

Note 3

Tuesday morn

Dear Jack & Babies,

I think Willie still improves, the dr. comes only once a day now. But he says this will be a very hard week on him. He says Will must be kept very quiet this week and not try to get up any as he might have a chill.

He says he likes his lungs to heal pretty well before he leaves bed, if not it is liable to leave a cronic ailment.

Willie has coughed more last night than usual. If I can possibly stay with him this week his worst will be over.

You know how hard it is for the rest of them to be careful. They mean to be and think they are but they miss the mark.

Papa sat up until 12 last night, the first night Isaac or I left him.

I can emagine what a time you are having at home. I hope you get along with the childrens clothes alright. I know I left them in bad shape.

Note 4

Saturday

Dear Jack, babies and all the rest of you,

I just received Jack's letter and it makes me feel so badly to think of poor Pearl being so sick. I am more glad than

I can tell, that Dolly is with her and Mother. I feel sure she will get well now. Tell Pearl, for me, how sorry I am that I cannot be with her some of the time too, But poor Willie is so sick! And they all, even the Dr., depends on me so much I don't know how I could leave him. The Dr says he needs a woman's care and although I do not understand all, I do all I can, the best I can. I really think that Willie is on the improve but you know how hard it is for one as sick as he is to feel much change. The Dr says the disease generally runs from 2 to 4 weeks.

Am anxious to hear from you again.

Willie has begun to eat mush & drink milk. I think he will gain a little strength. I do hope Pearl is gaining poor girl.

I hope dear you are taking good care of your cold. I feel fine. It just seems strength is given me.

Well dearest I want to send this to Richardson's early so it will have every chance to get off. It is very hard to get them written and sent.

With best love to all and kisses for my little ones and Papa.

I am as ever your devoted

wife & Mama.

Note 5

My dear little babies,

Mama thinks of you all the time and hopes you are being good and helping all you can. I know how much those dear little hands help Mama and I want them to help others just the same.

I am going to send some medicine for the lumps on the childrens necks. The Dr. says they shouldn't be allowed to remain any longer than possible—especially Earl's.

If you need me with the children, Jack, you know I must go home. I know your judgment is clearer than mine and I'll depend on you for advise. I am writing this in hopes it will be sent this afternoon but in case it don't I will mail it tomorrow.

Tell Dolly I am very glad indeed that she is better.

Give my love to all and remember how anxious I am to hear from you.

Lovingly,

Katie

Note 6

Monday
morning

Dear Jack.

Willie is getting along nicely. Coughed a good deal towards morning and does not feel quite so well. But his pulse & temperature are good and he is going alright. I had a letter over at Richardsons all day yesterday but they had no chance to send it. Frank will take this to the train men for me this morning.

I'll try to find out, from Dr. today, how soon I can be spared. I was so glad to get your letter yesterday and know you were all well.

This will be quite a budget[106] of a letter when you get it.

---

[106] Used in its original meaning of a bag or pouch with its contents: hence, a collection of items.

I've been writing every day since I've been here and have not got any off. You should get two today.

Love to all

Katie

*Written on the same sheet of paper*

Dear Addie.

I was so glad to get your sweet little letter and know you were all so well and I noticed too how nicely it was written. Grandpa enjoyed your letter very much and will answer as soon as he can.

Mama would like to be with you today Earley boy. Papa must let me know how I am to get home.

And little Edith I suppose you Minnie and Earl just have a lovely time.

All of you help poor Grandma all you can. Give her my love, also Aunt Dolly, Pearl, Uncle Frank and all the rest.

Kisses to Papa & babies

Your loving<br>Mama

Willie recovered and Katie went home to Calabasas.

# School Days for the Haas Children

*Calabasas School, built in 1890*

Dear Addie
Out in the wilds
a flower grew, smiling and
sweet that flower was you.
With kind thoughts
Your teacher
C. Mac Dermott

Dear Daughter,
May every blessing
God can give
Bring peace around you
While you live.

3-13-04
Mama.

165

The changes which technology wrought in the lives of 20th century Americans have been subject for libraries of learned works. These changes came slowly to Calabasas and almost not at all to the Haases during their remaining years in the area. Addie remembers that when the first car appeared on the road, the teacher let them leave their seats and go to the windows to see it. Because they were remote from the nearest railroad line, they had not had the advantage of the wireless for communication. There was no light and power, no telephone; they remained, technologically speaking, in the 19th century.

One item was available to them, however, and in using it, they were able to record their family history in a modern way. This was the invention of the small portable camera, the Kodak, which allowed every man to become his own photographer and removed picture-taking from the realm of a rare and solemn moment when the subjects sat in their best clothes with grim and frozen expressions to a more casual and frequent occurrence. Katie, in 1895, had been impressed enough to write to Jack when a photographer took a picture of Frank Perret in the field with his work clothes on, but by 1906 she was taking pictures of her own daughters in their bathing suits. Katie never had a bathing suit as a child, but if she had, photographing her in it would have been unthinkable.

Thus for the Haas children there exists a visual documentation of their childhood. What follows is a collection of verbal snapshots, glimpses of their early years. They are Addie's recollections: some imparted in

166

conversations on tape with her daughter, Catherine; others remembered from earlier times by Catherine.

## The Haas Home in Calabasas

Catherine:  (examining with her mother, Addie, the photograph of the John Haas Home Place)

I have a memory—as if I'd been in that house when I was a girl -with you and Aunt Edith. We'd been on some kind of an outing and we stopped on the way home. It was abandoned and boarded up. That would have been in the early '30s.

Addie:  It could have been.

Catherine:  For instance, was there wallpaper in the house? I have this faint recollection of Aunt Edith saying, "Why, our old wallpaper's still here!"

Addie:  I think our bedrooms were papered. And the dining room had a ceiling finished with tongue-and-groove. Natural wood but varnished over.

Catherine:  How many rooms did you have?

Addie:  We had a living room and dining room across the front. Off the dining room was a bedroom (my mother's and father's), a little hall with a large closet, and another bedroom (Edith's and mine). We had one side of the closet, and Mama and Papa had the other. Later, on the west wall of that closet my father put in an old galvanized bathtub. Of course, there was no bathroom in the house. Up until that time we took baths in an old round wash tub in the kitchen. When Earl got a little bit bigger, they built on another room clear across the west side of the building—the full length. My mother used the front half as a sewing room and the back half was Earl's bedroom. There was an outside door at the back of that bedroom. At the back of the living room was another bedroom—a guest bedroom.

Catherine: Where was the kitchen?

Addie: The kitchen was back of the dining room. Outside the kitchen on the back wall to the left as you went out, I remember they had a long shelf where the men all used to go to wash. And then—it was like a breezeway—which led to a little stone house where we kept our milk and perishables. Potatoes and everything of that sort because we didn't have refrigeration. Then in the yard on the west side was the woodpile and the clothesline. There was a little pit out there in that yard where my mother'd start a fire to heat the wash water. To take our baths the only water we had was what was heated in a tank at the back of the wood stove. We'd get a bath Saturday night.

Catherine: Did you have pitchers of water and face bowls in your bedrooms?

Addie: No. We had a little shelf in the kitchen with a little mirror and a wash basin. We had a little galvanized sink on the wall where we'd get the water to wash our hands and face.

Catherine: Where was the privy?

Addie: Up on a little hill and down at the back of the hill

at the bottom of the hill there was a little—very small—stream of water, and about two-thirds of the way down the hill was the privy. A two-seater. I know when I was giving a talk at women's club I said I thought we learned good powers of retention. I can remember how we hated to walk down that hill in the cold weather—rain—or when it was hot.

Catherine: You'd sure think twice before you—

Addie: You just learned to wait and hold. It was a two-holer. Oh, and some Sears Roebuck catalog between the seats for toilet paper. That's what we had. (They laugh)

Catherine: Did the men board or live with you?

Addie: Well, on the east side of the house was a bunkhouse. And down the side of the little creek back of the bunkhouse, my father had a blacksmith shop. He had a forge and quite a lot of equipment. He shod all our horses. He did any blacksmith work that had to be done for the ranch.

Catherine: So you were a pretty self-sustaining operation?

Addie: Yes. We were.

Catherine: Now you must have had a little vegetable patch?

Addie: No. Old adobe. Not enough water.

Catherine: So did you have much fresh fruit or vegetables? You were talking last night about what a treat it was when your father returned from a trip for supplies with a crate of fresh cherries and how

|  |  |
|---|---|
|  | you were all allowed to eat them until they were gone. |
| Addie: | We'd get fresh fruit from Grandpa Ijams down at Studio City and my mother would can it. |
| Catherine: | I remember your telling—you kids and Grandpa Haas sitting all day long— |
| Addie: | —peeling fruit for canning. |
| Catherine: | I remember you telling me—and it surprised me, because I always thought of Calabasas as so dry and infertile—about mushrooms in the spring. |
| Addie: | Well, after it'd rain. This would be between the house and the bottom of the hill. Of course, the hill's gone now—practically—because the freeway went up higher, but the old road was lower. |
|  | There evidently at one time had been a pasture a horse corral or something -and after a rain, we'd go down there and gather mushrooms. But that was only in the winter after we'd had a good rain. |
| Catherine: | So your diet then was meat and potatoes? |
| Addie: | Well, meat, potatoes and canned vegetables. Lots of beans, potatoes, macaroni. I can remember Esther Mesa—she used to work for Mama when there were a lot of men to cook for she was later Esther Coig—Esther would say to Mama: "What'll it be tonight—potatoes or mac?" (They laugh) |

## Coffee

Addie:     Out in the little stone house I mentioned, Mama kept coffee. Arbuckle Coffee. The beans came in little packages with prize coupons. We kids ground the coffee and whoever ground the coffee got the prize coupon. I don't know what we ever got, but it was one job we battled for.

## Mama

Addie:     Grandpa Haas and Mama used to get into it sometimes. Once he said to her, "Katie, when my John met you, you were in rags, and look at you now."

Catherine:     (laughing) She was probably standing over a wood stove cooking at the time.

Addie:     Yes. And not only for the family but a baling crew as well. My mother worked. In the heat of summer—during the threshing season—she cooked for the work crews. She'd cook the meal on the wood stove, pack it on the wagon, go out and run down Old Dutch and hitch him up, and then drive the two or three miles—wherever the men were—serve the meal—drive home and clean up—just in time to start the evening meal.

One time we children were playing cards and got to quarreling. Mama came over, picked up the cards and threw them all into the wood stove.

Sundays, when we were little, Mama would hitch Old Dutch to the buggy and drive us to the schoolhouse on the Liberty Grade at Las

171

*At the Haas home place*

*Edith and Earl*

*Addie and Grandpa Haas*

Virgenes Canyon, about five miles away, for Sunday school. She and Mrs. Tweedy taught the classes. Then she'd bring us home and start the Sunday dinner.

### Addie's First Day of School, 1903

Addie, aged seven, is ready for her first day of school. Fresh clothes, a new straw hat, excited, anxious, she is suddenly dashed when her mother tells her that she must walk the two miles to school alone. Frightened but stoic, she sets out on the hot dusty and suddenly unfamiliar road. The wind, as if in league with the uncaring mother, lifts up her new hat and sails it down the embankment to the dry wash below.

Loss and panic by the roadside. Her new hat in the dust and brush. Hopeless thoughts rush at her: *get help go home... be late for school maybe get spanked.*

Hoof sounds on the road. Papa! Papa on his horse—scrambles down, retrieves the hat, gathers her up and rides her on to her first day of school. [107]

## Music Lessons

Addie:    We first had an old pump organ, and later Papa traded two horses for an upright piano. Edith and I went on Saturdays to take piano lessons from Mrs. Hub Russell who lived on the Workman Ranch. Hub Russell was Joe Russell's older brother. We left on our horses right after lunch—it took all afternoon—and the horses we were riding had more musical talent than either Edith or I.

## Hoboes

Addie:    We used to get lots of hoboes walking through because this was the main road through to—dirt road, of course—on the way to Ventura, and they used to come to the back door for a handout, and I never knew my mother to refuse one. She always gave them a sandwich or something. And I remember two incidents so clearly. One time, the old fellow came and she gave him his

---

[107] My version of a story told me when I was very young. It affected me deeply and I have never forgotten it.

handout—it was late in the afternoon and he said, "And now, my good lady, you can show me to my bed." My father used to let them sleep in the barn these hoboes. And to this day I wonder how it never got burned down. I guess they couldn't afford cigarettes. And the other time was—let's see—oh—this old fellow had been coming for years. About once a year he'd stop for a handout, and my mother would give it to him. And the last time he was there he said, "This is the last time you'll see me." And it was.

Catherine: There was no sense of fear?

Addie: No no. they were just walking through.

Catherine: In exchange for this, did they do a chore?

Addie: No. Just wanted something to eat — a free meal—

Catherine: —a real handout.

Addie: And Joe Russell used to tell about his mother doing the same thing up on the Russell Ranch in the Conejo. I think they had certain places they knew they'd always get something to eat. He said his mother always fed them.

## Two Memories of Christmas in Calabasas

Addie: There was the time we were having a big Christmas celebration at home—with the tree for us children. And Uncle Ike was brought in

175

to be Santa Claus with a red suit and a cotton beard. We kids were all waiting in another room for them to open the doors so we'd see the tree and Santa, and we waited and we waited. What we didn't know was that Uncle Ike's whiskers had caught fire from a candle on the Christmas tree, and he and the men were busy putting the fire out. Santa never came that year.

A letter to her ten-year-old granddaughter, Katie Hurley, from Addie Haas Mulholland:

Christmas 1970

Dear Katie:

When I was your age, we lived on a ranch in Calabasas. We did not have electric lights nor furnaces. In fact, we didn't even have fire-places to keep us warm.

My mother cooked on a big wood stove and we had a little wood heater in the dining room.

As Christmas time drew near, my sister, brother and I would sit at the dining room table and choose the gifts we wanted from a Sears Roebuck catalogue. After a lot of crossing out and adding on to our list, we handed it to our mother and waited impatiently for Christmas morning.

We did not have automobiles when I was your age. Everyone rode or drove horses. My father pastured horses on our ranch for a livery stable in Pasadena. Among the horses there were always some donkeys which Papa would let us ride bareback.

*Las Virgenes Canyon, 1906. Addie (standing) and Edith in bathing suits*

On the Christmas I am telling you about Edith, Earl and I decided we would each ask for a child's saddle that we saw pictured in a Sears Roebuck catalogue. Our fondest hope was that we would get one saddle to "take turns" riding.

*Addie on Jeff, a roan*

*On the way to Warner's Hot Springs, Summer 1911. At right are Ruth Schneider Allen, a friend, and Edith on the Indian ponies, Pima and Chapo*

*Life in the open*

Imagine our surprise on Christmas morning when we awoke to find beside each of our beds a beautiful new saddle draped over the back of a chair with a shiny new bridle hanging beside it.

Boys and girls have so much more in the way of expensive gifts today but I do not think any children could have greater joy or more love for their parents than we had that Christmas on our ranch.

It is still one of the happy memories I have of my childhood when we lived without any "modern conveniences."

Merry Christmas,

Grandma

*John and Katie Haas (in second row) in a Packard sight-seeing bus, Seattle, Washington, August 1909*

When Valentin Haas was told that there were plans afoot to lay out a town site in the area now known as Canoga Park, he said in one of his rare but notable statements: "That's no place for a town. Too many big red ants." His warning went unheeded, however, and in 1911, the Los Angeles Suburban Homes Company, putting the Janss Company on the job, laid out a town called Owensmouth, now Canoga Park. The area was nowhere near the mouth of the Owens Valley Aqueduct which was then under construction and would be completed in 1913, but in the usual hyperbolic style of land developers, the name was given to suggest to the guileless that water would be abundant in the new community.[108] There were, however, other attractions offered and promises kept: new homes, schoolhouses and a great 150-foot boulevard running east and west for sixteen miles through the very heart of the San Fernando Valley (this became Sherman Way), along which the Pacific Electric Railway was to extend its tracks out through the Cahuenga Pass on to Van Nuys and terminate at Owensmouth. These prospects offered a strong incentive to a family with children of high-school age to leave Calabasas and take up residence in a nearby town which would provide them with some of the amenities of civilization. Jack and Katie were about to take a big step.

The customary practice of land developers in kicking off a new tract at that time was to throw a big barbecue and provide transportation to the site. In the same year that

[108] Owens Valley water did come to the San Fernando Valley in 1915 after an election in which Valley residents voted to join the city of Los Angeles.

Owensmouth was being readied for buyers, Paul Whitsett was directing an even larger production in the opening of the new settlement of Van Nuys. In his biography are some interesting details of how such a show was put on. These early land men were worthy forerunners of Cecil B. deMille and his Hollywood epics. Consider the following:

> In January, 1911… Mr. Harry Chandler asked Mr. Whitsett when he expected to start the town of Van Nuys. [Whitsett demurred and tossed the question back to Chandler.] Chandler replied, "I think the 22nd day of February would be an excellent time to start the townsite. Let's put it on sale at that date.[109]

One full month to start a town! The mind boggles. Whitsett's did not, however, and flaring into action he proceeded to set up a sales and advertising organization in downtown Los Angeles, fight and win a battle with the Southern Pacific Railroad for a reduced passenger fare from Los Angeles to Van Nuys (he had prematurely advertised a 25¢ round trip in the *Los Angeles Times*, the Southern Pacific wanted $1, and refusing to change the advertisement, Whitsett got a compromised fare of 50 cents, he himself assuming whatever loss it might entail), and make arrangements for a barbecue to feed ten thousand people. When he began to doubt that his advertising efforts would attract that many people, he hit on the idea of what must have been one of the pioneer ventures in the use of the telephone for soliciting.

"I sent for my advertising man and told him that I wanted him to invite everybody in Southern California who had a telephone, to attend the opening of this new town."

---

[109] Merle Armitage, *Success is No Accident: The Biography of William Paul Whitsett*, Yucca Valley, CA, Manzanita Press, 1959. pp. 116-120. The following three paragraphs are from the same source and same pages.

At the cost of a nickel a call everybody in Southern California with a telephone was invited, and thousands accepted. On February 22, 1911, fifteen thousand people arrived on the barren plain that was to be Van Nuys, ate prodigious quantities of barbecue and bought $250,000 worth of lots. At one point in the proceedings, there was such a mob that Joe Romero, the barbecue king, in charge of the barbecue, said, "Whitsett, you've got more than ten thousand people here, maybe there are fifteen thousand, and I don't have food enough for them." I suggested he give them less beans, cut the meat a little finer. "I'll be out of buns," he complained. I said we would send someone over to North Hollywood to get some bread. We sent a car, which finally came back with a lot of bread in the back seat.[110]

The Haas family attended a similar barbecue at the opening of the town of Owensmouth. At this one there was no food shortage, but for many of the guests it must have been the grittiest meal they ever ate because on that day the famous north wind of the San Fernando Valley chose to blow. Because all the land was open plain, there was nothing to stop the dust and sand from flying onto food plates and into open mouths. The Haases were no strangers to the wind, though, so undeterred by a little dirt, they bought ten acres of land and a house at the southwest corner of Shoup and Vanowen Streets and prepared to move up in the world.

At this point, Addie, who had been the first to leave Calabasas, was sixteen and had been attending Pasadena High School for two years. Edith, fourteen, had followed for her freshman year, while Earl, aged twelve, remained at home and went to grammar school. The move was momentous for

---

[110] Whitsett, p. 120.

all of them. Jack, at forty-five, had spent twenty-four years of good and bad times in Calabasas, and Katie, thirty-five years old, could look back on her twenty-seven years of life there, remembering that in that place she had grown to womanhood, lost her beloved sister Nettie, fallen in love, married and borne her children. She could one day say of her life in Calabasas what Gertrude Stein had said of hers in Oakland: that it was "the half that made me."

In the fall of 1912 they moved to their new house. It was two storied and had an exterior of dark brown clapboard, with brick chimney and supports of brickwork for the front porch and driveway. Upstairs there were two bedrooms and a long room across the front of the house. On the ground floor were a living room, dining room, two bedrooms, one bathroom and a kitchen. The kitchen had an electric stove, an advanced and luxurious piece of equipment after a lifetime of cooking on a wood stove. There was an icebox with ice delivered to the house. There was a screen porch where they put their old dining room table from Calabasas, and in the dining room they enjoyed new oak Mission-style furniture. Katie, after a life as a pioneer woman, was about to become a suburban matron.

The move to Owensmouth, embryonic as the town was, produced more profound change in the lives of the women than in those of the men. The inexorable domestic tasks such as providing wood for the stove and pumping water were to be no more. Jack's work continued unchanged, and although he could enjoy the increased comfort of his new home, his workday was unaltered. Katie, on the other hand, was to find new uses for her time which would draw her to the genteel life of the middle-class American woman.

In the years ahead she would join with other women in a women's club, which immediately organized the first library in Owensmouth, she became active in the affairs of the Methodist Community Church, and she was able to garden for ornamental purposes. Photographs show the house in 1912 surrounded by bare dirt, but in 1915, a snapshot shows a lawn, shrubs and flowers. There had never been either time or water for such an activity in Calabasas.

For Addie and Edith the move must have been a joyous one. After two less than glorious years with Grandma Perret in Pasadena, Addie was able to leave behind her the twice-cooked pancakes, the Victorian horsehair furniture and marble-top tables which she loathed, and the feeling of being a second-class citizen ("She used to make me feel like a servant."). Edith, who had lived only one year with her grandmother, may not have felt so intensely negative but was nonetheless happy to return to Mama and Papa. The increased space and privacy of their new home, the indoor bathroom and the Mission furniture, which was all the thing in 1912, must have elated them. In the fall both girls entered Hollywood High School (the Owensmouth High School was still under construction), riding the big red cars of the Pacific Electric line with other young people of the town. Edith was to meet her future husband on one of those rides to town, and Addie—but enough! All those stories must be told at a future time. The Calabasas days are over.

# Index

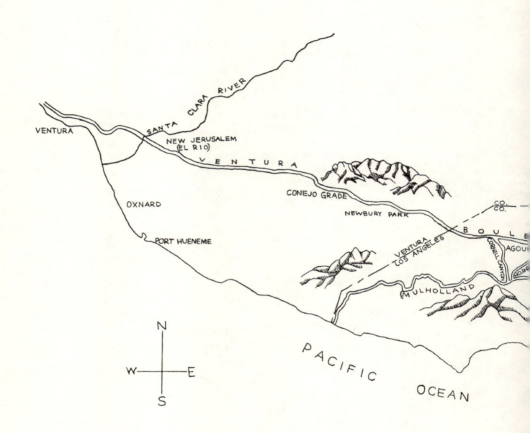

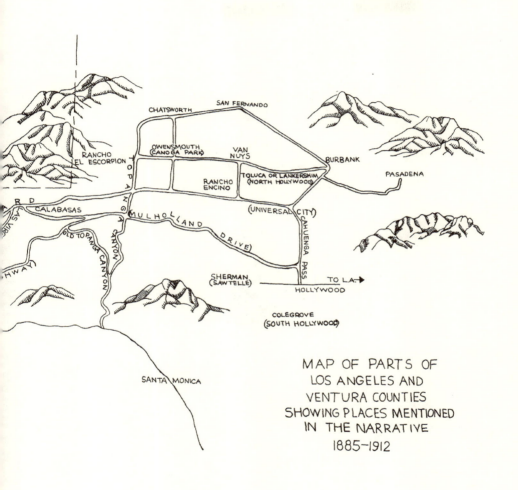

MAP OF PARTS OF
LOS ANGELES AND
VENTURA COUNTIES
SHOWING PLACES MENTIONED
IN THE NARRATIVE
1885-1912